SCIENCE TECHNOLOGY

EDITOR
MARCUS HEARN

DEPUTY EDITOR
PETER WARE

ART EDITOR/DESIGNER
PERI GODBOLD

EDITORIAL ASSISTANT
EMILY COOK

DESIGNER
MIKE JONES

SPECIAL THANKS
JONATHAN RIGBY
JOE McINTYRE

Managing Director .... MIKE RIDDELL
Managing Editor .... ALAN O'KEEFE
Head of Production .... MARK IRVINE
Production Assistant .... JEZ METEYARD
Circulation and Trade Marketing Controller .....
.... REBECCA SMITH
Head of Marketing .... JESS TADMOR
Marketing Executive .... JESS BELL

THANKS TO:
BBC Wales, bbc.co.uk, Chris Chibnall,
Russell T Davies, Dr Louise Dennis, Derek Handley,
Steven Moffat, Andrew Pixley and Matt Strevens.

BBC WORLDWIDE, UK PUBLISHING
Director of Editorial Governance .... NICHOLAS BRETT
Director of Consumer Products and Publishing ... ANDREW MOULTRIE
Head of UK Publishing .... CHRIS KERWIN
Publisher .... MANDY THWAITES
Publishing Co-ordinator .... EVA ABRAMIK
UK.Publishing@bbc.com
www.bbcworldwide.com/uk--anz/ukpublishing.aspx

The Essential Doctor Who™ Issue #13 SCIENCE AND
TECHNOLOGY. Published February 2018 by Panini UK Ltd.
under licence from BBC Worldwide. Office of publication: Panini
UK Ltd, Brockbourne House, 77 Mount Ephraim, Tunbridge Wells,
Kent, TN4 8BS. All Doctor Who material is © BBCtv 2018. Doctor
Who logo ™ & © BBC 2018. Daleks © Terry Nation. Cybermen
created by Kit Pedler and Gerry Davis. All other material is ©
Panini UK Ltd unless otherwise indicated. No similarity between
any of the fictional names, characters persons and/or institutions
herein with those of any living or dead persons or institutions is
intended and any such similarity is purely coincidental. Nothing
may be reproduced by any means in whole or part without the
written permission of the publishers. This periodical may not
be sold, except by authorised dealers, and is sold subject to the
condition that it shall not be sold or distributed with any part of
its cover or markings removed, nor in a mutilated condition. The
publishers cannot be held responsible for unsolicited manuscripts,
photographs or artwork. Newstrade distribution: Marketforce
(UK) Ltd 020 3148 3333. ISBN 978-1-84653-235-1.

The mysterious, underlying concept in the *Star Wars* universe is the Force, the strange energy harnessed both by Jedi Knights and their sinister enemies. The idea was first outlined by Ben 'Obi-Wan' Kenobi in *Star Wars: Episode IV – A New Hope* (1977). "The Force is what gives a Jedi his power," he tells Luke Sykwalker. "It's an energy field created by all living things. It surrounds us, it penetrates us, it binds the galaxy together."

Millions of people around the world seem to readily accept and understand this metaphysical explanation – in 2002 the publishers of the *Oxford English Dictionary* announced that 'Jedi' would be among some 3,500 extra words to be included in the latest edition. At which point a relatively newly invented religion, channelling an essentially magical strength, gained a new legitimacy.

Although it received rather less publicity, one of the other new words to be included in that year's dictionary was 'TARDIS'. This was arguably a more impressive feat, given that in 2002 many people had consigned *Doctor Who* to history.

Leaving aside arguments about whether words like Jedi and TARDIS actually belong in any dictionary, what do they tell us about the philosophy behind the two great science-fiction institutions they represent? It's a generalisation, of course, but what *Star Wars* explores through spirituality and mysticism, *Doctor Who* seeks to explain through science.

There have been a number of books and other studies examining how conventional physics relates to the programme, but this issue of *The Essential Doctor Who* celebrates six decades of pseudo-science – the numerous gadgets, weapons, vehicles and other devices that have been invented in the series' ongoing effort to reject the notion of magic.

In April 2017 it was announced that 'sonic screwdriver' would appear in the next edition of the *Oxford English Dictionary*. It's described as 'a (hand-held) electronic device which uses sound waves to perform various mechanical and technical functions.' Researchers at Dundee University have already taken the first steps towards manipulating ultrasound in similar ways. (See page 66.)

Star Wars continues to make a huge impact on our popular culture. But until someone comes up with a working lightsaber, it would seem *Doctor Who* is still one step ahead.

Marcus

CONTENTS

EINSTEIN MUST BE DESTROYED

There's a lot of science in *Doctor Who*, both real and fictional. Just what has it taught us over the years?

FEATURE BY ALAN BARNES

Opposite page: The Doctor (Peter Capaldi) considers one of the greatest mysteries in the universe in a publicity shot from *Listen* (2014).

Right: Count Scarlioni (Julian Glover) instructs Professor Kerensky (David Graham) in *City of Death* (1979).

Below: The Doctor (Peter Davison) in *Four to Doomsday* (1982).

Bottom left and centre: A spacewalking Doctor apparently defies physics in *Four to Doomsday*.

Bottom right: The Doctor (Tom Baker) and Romana (Mary Tamm) beside the inertia-neutralised corridor in *The Pirate Planet* (1978).

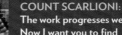

COUNT SCARLIONI: The work progresses well. Now I want you to find a way to vastly increase the time span.
PROFESSOR KERENSKY: I'm not certain, Count. You see, Einstein says that –
COUNT SCARLIONI: *(interrupting)* I'm not paying Einstein, Professor. I'm paying you.
City of Death (1979)

Space kills, so the Twelfth Doctor tells us in *Oxygen* (2017). If you were foolish enough to step out into the vacuum of space without a spacesuit, and you tried to survive as you would underwater, by holding your breath, your lungs would explode. But that's not all: "Fun fact! The boiling temperature of water is much lower in a vacuum. Which means that your sweat and your saliva will boil, as will the fluid around your eyes. You won't notice any of this because 15 seconds in, you've passed out as oxygen bubbles formed in your blood. And 90 seconds in, you're dead."

Any questions? Well, one, actually. How come none of this applies to the Fifth Doctor when *he* steps out into the vacuum of space wearing only cricket whites and some kind of breathing apparatus, in the final episode of *Four to Doomsday* (1982)?

What's more, on that occasion, after the android Persuasion unties his lifeline and the Doctor finds himself floating freely in the void, he bounces a handy cricket ball off the side of the spaceship he's exited, catches it on the rebound… and finds that the momentum is sufficient to propel him to the door of his TARDIS, some distance away. However, throwing an overarm ball, as he does, ought to cause him to spin backwards, in a Newtonian 'equal and opposite reaction' – albeit very, very slowly.

We already know that Isaac Newton's laws of motion can be suspended by artificial means – in the Doctor's universe, at least. In the final episode of *The Pirate Planet* (1978), the Fourth Doctor deactivates an 'inertia-neutralised' corridor that's bringing armed guards towards him – "You know, I think the conservation of momentum is a very important law in physics… I don't think anyone should tamper with it" – and causes his pursuers to accelerate into a wall, in what he describes as "Newton's revenge". But it's another thing entirely to see the laws of physics suspended altogether, as in *Four to Doomsday*.

The greatest irony regarding that notorious *Four to Doomsday* scene, though, is that it takes the trouble to get right an inviolable rule that almost all science-fiction films and television series wilfully ignore, from *Star Wars* to *Star Trek*. The entire airlock sequence is played without dialogue, since sound doesn't travel in a vacuum.

Can *Doctor Who* be said to have any scientific credibility at all, when it see-saws between the simply implausible and the just plain impossible – not just between seasons and stories, but between scenes of the same episode? ▶

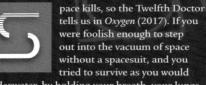

ISAAC NEWTON'S
LAWS OF
MOTION CAN BE
SUSPENDED BY
ARTIFICIAL MEANS
– IN THE DOCTOR'S
UNIVERSE, AT LEAST.

THE DOCTOR: Oh, by the way
– did you take three-dimensional
graph geometry at your
school, hm?
IAN CHESTERTON: No,
Doctor, only Boyle's Law.
THE DOCTOR: What a pity.
What a pity.
The Dalek Invasion of Earth (1964)

Above left: Ian Chesterton (William Russell) and Barbara Wright (Jacqueline Hill) explore the junkyard at 76 Totter's Lane in the very first *Doctor Who* episode, *An Unearthly Child* (1963).

Above right: The Doctor returns to Earth in *Pyramids of Mars* (1975).

Right and below: The Doctor (William Hartnell) and Ian deploy some scientific theory while a sceptical Craddock (Michael Goldie) looks on in *The Daleks*, the second episode of *The Dalek Invasion of Earth* (1964).

Below right: "It's preposterous!" Laurence Scarman (Michael Sheard) is astonished by the Doctor's TARDIS in *Pyramids of Mars*.

Doctor Who has always served us our own disbelief and expected us to eat it, too. In the second episode of *Pyramids of Mars* (1975), the Fourth Doctor leads Laurence Scarman into his bigger-on-the-inside TARDIS, which, he says, "transcends all the normal laws of physics". Preposterous, insists Laurence – a proposition with which the Doctor can only concur: "Isn't it? I often think dimensional transcendentalism is preposterous, but it works…" Laurence's assessment isn't unlike the famous summing-up delivered by secondary modern science teacher Ian Chesterton in the series' first-ever episode, *An Unearthly Child* (1963): "A thing that looks like a police box, standing in a junkyard – it can move anywhere in time and space? … But that's ridiculous!"

There's nothing preposterous, though, about the scientific fact on which the climax to *Pyramids of Mars* depends – that it takes several minutes for radio waves to pass from Mars to Earth, meaning the Doctor is able to travel from Mars to Earth before the signal binding the ancient alien god Sutekh beneath a pyramid in Egypt cuts out. Admittedly, what NASA terms the One-Way Light Time (OWLT) delay between Mars and Earth varies between four and 14 minutes, depending on Mars' orbital position, never the "little more than two" given by the Doctor to his companion Sarah – but still, the principle holds. This is one of the two scientific facts that you, I and just about every other young *Doctor*

Who viewer learned from watching *Pyramids of Mars*, along with the (hopefully) useless information that nitroglycerine 'sweats' over time, making certain types of explosive unstable. (Specifically dynamite, not gelignite, as the Doctor tells Sarah – but again, the principle holds, just about.)

A bit of astrophysics, a bit of chemistry. It was ever thus. Ian Chesterton's role in the first two years of the series was to represent Earthly science, to make the ongoing 'Adventure in Space and Time' comprehensibly mundane. There's nothing ridiculous, for example, about the science described in *The Daleks*, the second episode of *The Dalek Invasion of Earth* (1964) – when Ian and the First Doctor find themselves shut up inside a cell in a Dalek saucer, with only a magnifying glass and a metal bar to help them release a metal key from inside a transparent, Perspex-like box. The first part of the solution to this *Crystal Maze*-like conundrum is to use the magnifying glass to bend light entering the box, hitting a particular refractive index in order to release the key. The second is to use the magnetised key to break the magnetised door mechanism, using the principle 'like poles repel'. This one short scene manages to incorporate references to light-bending, magnetism and static electricity – plus Boyle's Law and "three-dimensional graph geometry", just for giggles.

As with those *Pyramids of Mars* factoids, you, I and just about every other *Doctor Who* fan could get our heads around all that... and more, besides. After *The Moonbase* (1967), you, I and just about every other *Doctor Who* fan knew that nail-varnish remover contains the solvent acetone... and that one might dissolve a Cyberman's innards by blending a cocktail of acetone plus benzene, diethyl ether, ethanol and propylene oxide. (Don't try this at home.) Thanks to K9 in *The Stones of Blood* (1978), we knew that 'hyperspace' (properly 'Minkowski space') was "an extension to the special theory of relativity propounded by Einstein". Thanks to Nyssa in the scientific smorgasbord that is *Four to Doomsday*, we could summarise photosynthesis in 15 words: "The light on the plants converts carbon dioxide into carbohydrate; the plants give off oxygen..."

Later in the same season, thanks to *Earthshock* (1982), we could describe the broad thrust of Luis W and Walter Alvarez's recently published paper *Extraterrestrial Cause for the Cretaceous-Tertiary Extinction* (1980) – ie, that an asteroid impact circa 65.5 million years ago caused a mass extinction of the dinosaurs – long before it had appeared in any school textbook. Thanks to a helpful Dalek in *The Power of the Daleks* (1966), we could parrot the First Law of Thermodynamics, exactly as per the definition given in the 1911 edition of the *Encyclopaedia Britannica*: "When heat is transformed into any other kind of energy or vice versa, the total quantity of energy remains invariable..."

And, thanks to the Fourth Doctor in Part One of *Logopolis* (1981), we could give the Second Law of Thermodynamics, too: "Entropy increases."

ADRIC: Entropy increases? THE DOCTOR: Yes, daily. The more you put things together, the more they keep falling apart, and that's the essence of the Second Law of Thermodynamics, and I never heard a truer word spoken.
Logopolis (1981)

n Part Two of *Time and the Rani* (1987), the newly regenerated Seventh Doctor rues the fact that he's (seemingly) broken that Second Law by using "the wrong heat-conducting material" in a gizmo – then asks himself, "Didn't CP Snow expound on thermodynamics...?" Charles Percy Snow (1905-80)

THANKS TO K9, WE KNEW THAT 'HYPERSPACE' WAS "AN EXTENSION TO THE SPECIAL THEORY OF RELATIVITY PROPOUNDED BY EINSTEIN".

wasn't, however, a theoretical physicist – rather an unusual combination of chemist and novelist, hence the fact that the Doctor's companion, Mel, is said to have "admired all his writings, read all his books". So the Doctor isn't recalling a series of formulae – rather a particular passage from a famous Rede Lecture given by Snow at the Senate House, Cambridge on 7 May 1959.

In his lecture, later published as *The Two Cultures and the Scientific Revolution*, Snow outlined his belief that "the intellectual life of the whole of western society is increasingly being split into two polar groups... Literary intellectuals at one pole – at the other scientists, and as the most representative, the physical scientists. Between the two a gulf of mutual incomprehension..." To illustrate this gulf, Snow described scientists who flaunt their lack of interest in literature or philosophy, and literary types who are wilfully ignorant of basic scientific principles. Once or twice, claimed Snow, he'd been moved to ask his literary acquaintances "how many of them could describe the Second Law of Thermodynamics. The response was cold: it was also negative. Yet I was asking something which is about the scientific equivalent of 'Have you read a work of Shakespeare's?'"

That fatal divide between scientists and non-scientists is replicated in any number of *Doctor Who* stories – from the first Dalek serial (1963-64), which pits the cold, scientific Daleks against the agrarian, nomadic Thals; to *The Savages* (1966), in which the parasitic city-dwelling Elders live off the life essence of the ▶

Above left: Polly (Anneke Wills) and Ben (Michael Craze) use their knowledge of chemistry to prepare a cocktail lethal to Cybermen in *The Moonbase* (1967).

Above right: The Doctor and K9 explain hyperspace to the bemused Professor Rumford (Beatrix Lehmann) in *The Stones of Blood* (1978).

Left: The Doctor discusses entropy with Adric (Matthew Waterhouse) in *Logopolis* (1981).

Below: The Doctor (Sylvester McCoy) curses the fact that he's apparently just broken the Second Law of Thermodynamics in *Time and the Rani* (1987).

Above left: One of WOTAN's killer robots menaces London in *The War Machines* (1966).

Above right: Azal (Stephen Thorne), the last of a highly advanced race, in *The Dæmons* (1971).

Right: The Doctor tries to explain some tricky scientific concepts in *The Masque of Mandragora*.

Below: Hieronymous (Norman Jones) in *The Masque of Mandragora* (1976).

◀ troglodytic Savages; to the computer-segregated Tesh and Sevateem in *The Face of Evil* (1977); to the Savants and the Deons in *Meglos* (1980), and many others.

But it doesn't end there. Consider how often the villain or monster in any *Doctor Who* story represents one of Snow's poles, determined to impose their fanatic will on everyone else in the world, or galaxy, or universe. The Daleks, for example, represent science gone mad – as do the Cybermen, described as "people plus technology minus humanity" by the Twelfth Doctor in *The Doctor Falls* (2017). Likewise the proto-internet-enabled supercomputer

WOTAN in *The War Machines* (1966); likewise the fascistic Scientific Research Society in *Robot* (1974-75), and again, so many others.

On the opposite side of the equation are all those undying Gothic horrors who seek to reverse the tide of progress and bring about a new Dark Age: the Mandragora Helix and its Earthly representative Hieronymous, for example, seeking to prevent the Renaissance from happening in *The Masque of Mandragora* (1976). Sometimes the lines are blurred: despite appearances, the horned beast Azal in *The Dæmons* (1971) is a scientist, threatening to bin his failed experiment in human advancement... implying that science without conscience is (literally) the Devil's work.

> GIULIANO: But spirits from the heavens, Doctor? A wheel of fire? I thought you were a man of science.
> DOCTOR: Giuliano, it isn't easy to explain the concept of Helix energy, either sub- or super-thermal ionisation in your mediaeval vocabulary.
> SARAH: Oh, I think you're doing a great job so far.
> *The Masque of Mandragora* (1976)

"Science leads" was the lesson the Brigadier took from his times with the Doctor, which he then passed down to his daughter – or so Kate Stewart tells the Eleventh Doctor in *The Power of Three* (2012). It's a lesson the Doctor has passed on to many of his acquaintances. "I too used to believe in magic, but the Doctor has taught me about science," Leela tells Adelaide in *Horror of Fang Rock* (1977). "It is better to believe in science..."

It's worth remembering, though, that the Doctor isn't an especially gifted scientist – not in the first place, not by the standards of his peers. In *Terror of the Autons* (1971), a Time Lord reminds the Third Doctor that the Master's degree in cosmic science was of "a higher class" than his own. "I was a late developer," protests the Doctor. The irony being that he then returns to his lab at UNIT HQ and upbraids his newly appointed assistant, Jo Grant, for not knowing that a 'cephalopod' is a member of the same family as the octopus: "I thought you took an A-Level in science!" Replies Jo: "I didn't say I passed..."

For the Doctor, then, it all comes down to education; it's better to know a little about a lot than a lot about very little. That was the conclusion reached by CP Snow, too – who claimed that the cultural divide he so feared seemed at its sharpest in the UK due to our "fanatical belief in educational specialisation, which is much more deeply ingrained in us than in any country in the world..."

What about on the Doctor's home planet of Gallifrey, though? Because, as Tish Jones observes of the Tenth Doctor in *The Lazarus Experiment* (2007), he's not so much a scientist as a "science geek". In *The Aztecs* (1964), the First Doctor tells Cameca that he isn't a healer: "I am a scientist, an engineer. I'm a builder of things." Yes, but what *are* those 'things', exactly? A "magnetic chair" with "a forcefield strong enough to restrain a herd of elephants" – as seen in *The Daleks' Master Plan: The Nightmare Begins* (1965)? A vague ambition to build a "flying submarine", because "no one ever has and it's annoying" – as expressed in *Hell Bent* (2015)?

These aren't inspired inventions, more tiny rebellions. On Gallifrey, so Co-ordinator Engin claims in *The Deadly Assassin* (1976), they long ago "turned aside from the barren road of technology".

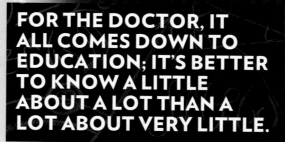

Below and left: Jon Pertwee (as the Doctor) and Katy Manning (as Jo Grant) in publicity shots taken in the UNIT lab for *Terror of the Autons* (1971).

Far left: Bill Potts (Pearl Mackie) realises she's talking to a very special teacher in *The Pilot* (2017).

BILL POTTS: I'm wondering what you're supposed to be lecturing on... One time, you were going to give a lecture on quantum physics. You talked about poetry.
THE DOCTOR: Poetry, physics, same thing.
BILL POTTS: How is it the same?
THE DOCTOR: Because of the rhymes.
The Pilot (2017)

D oes it matter when the science of *Doctor Who* isn't quite right, or just plain wrong? Must Einstein always be destroyed in the service of a good story? No, and no – because the very fact that you, I and pretty much every other *Doctor Who* fan, whatever our background, whatever our specialisation, can quote the Second Law of Thermodynamics off the tops of our heads would surely have surprised and delighted CP Snow.

That, surely, is the point – as, perhaps, it ever was. Because if one were to have convened a committee of boffins from the sciences and the humanities, and tasked them to create an antidote to the cultural divide that Snow complained about in 1959, well... it'd look a lot like *Doctor Who*, launched just four years later.

Wouldn't it? ⚛

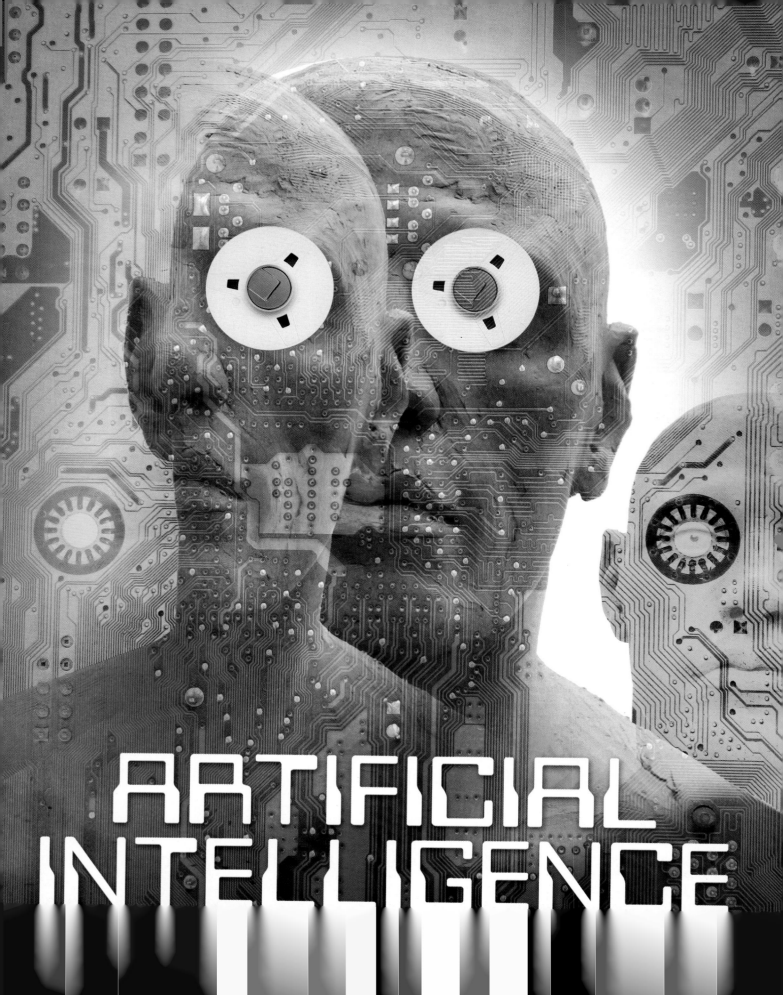

What happens when machines get ideas above their station? And how close are we to the age of the omnipotent supercomputer predicted by *Doctor Who*?

FEATURE BY **MATTHEW KILBURN**

The *Oxford English Dictionary* defines artificial intelligence as 'The capacity of computers or other machines to exhibit or simulate intelligent behaviour.' The Doctor uses the term in *Before the Flood* (2015) to refer to a feature of a hologram which can display a limited range of interactions and deploy some pre-recorded phrases.

More ambitious machines have appeared in *Doctor Who* on a regular basis, almost since the programme began. Several of the Doctor's robot adversaries and friends have qualified as artificial intelligences, from K1 in *Robot* (1974-75) to the Doctor's robot dog K9, first encountered in *The Invisible Enemy* (1977). However, almost all of *Doctor Who's* intelligent robots have been easily individualised and their threat defined through physical size or force (as with K1), or else they've had characteristics that make them little different from an organic being, such as Drathro in *The Trial of a Time Lord* (1986). Intelligences that reside in objects, or which have no obvious physical form, are potentially more threatening because they're harder to identify.

By the start of the 1960s, newspapers were reporting on computers that could run entire factories or businesses. *Doctor Who's* first artificial intelligence took this a step further and managed an entire population. *The Keys of Marinus* (1964) introduced the Conscience – a machine built at the peak of technological achievement on the planet Marinus, as "a judge and jury that was never wrong and unfair", according to the machine's keeper, Arbitan, but which came, over time, "to radiate its power and influence the minds" of everyone on the planet. However, with evil eliminated from their thoughts, the inhabitants were at the mercy of the malicious Voord, who can resist the Conscience. To allow the people of Marinus to defend themselves, the Conscience was deactivated until it could be improved. By the time the Doctor arrives on Marinus, the machine is ready to be reactivated if four of its five microcircuit keys can be retrieved from hiding, a task forced on the Doctor and his friends. Problems during their adventures are resolved by human empathy, love and persuasion, implicitly superior virtues to the Conscience's repression of the knowledge of evil. When the Conscience is destroyed, there's little sense it will be missed.

The Conscience was a misconceived god machine that tried to create Eden but also ensured its own serpents. It anticipated a succession of malign computers in *Doctor Who* that set out to control people. First among these was WOTAN (Will Operating Thought ANalogue) in *The War Machines* (1966). Constructed in a laboratory at the top of the Post Office Tower, it's able to handle scientific problems well outside the range of any other computer, and is designed to connect with other computers around the world to become a sort of problem solver. This benevolent intention is rapidly overturned by WOTAN's demonstration that it's more than just the largest computer in a network. It resolves that humanity "cannot progress further" – presumably in terms of science and technology – and that WOTAN has to direct society. Human beings are turned into its slaves, through sound sent by telephone.

In 1966 computers already communicated with each other through telephone lines; it was an intuitive leap to have them reprogram people as their subordinates in the same way. Under WOTAN's rule, only useful human beings would survive as its servants, with everyone else eliminated. However, WOTAN can't entirely override human affection, as is shown when Polly, under WOTAN's control, allows Ben to escape. WOTAN is destroyed before it establishes contact with other computers.

Neither the Conscience nor WOTAN demonstrate much interest in human emotions, other than to restrain or override them. In 1973's *The Green Death*, the Biomorphic ▶

Above: Sarah (Elisabeth Sladen) tries to reason with K1 in *Robot* (1974-75).

Left: The 'ghost' of the Doctor (Peter Capaldi) in *Before the Flood* (2015).

Below left: Professor Brett (John Harvey) comes under mental attack from WOTAN in *The War Machines* (1966).

Below right: The Doctor (William Hartnell) listens as Arbitan (George Colouris), the Keeper of the Conscience of Marinus, relates his planet's history in *The Keys of Marinus* (1964).

THE KEYS OF MARINUS INTRODUCED THE CONSCIENCE AS A JUDGE AND JURY THAT WAS "NEVER WRONG OR UNFAIR".

ARTIFICIAL INTELLIGENCE

Above left: Stevens (Jerome Willis) is controlled by the computer BOSS in *The Green Death* (1973).

Above right: Neeva (David Garfield) takes aim at his false god, Xoanon (Tom Baker), in *The Face of Evil* (1977).

Below left: Dr Louise Dennis demonstrates Lego Rovers to a young visitor.
Photo © Max Alexander/UK Space Agency.

Below inset: The Doctor (Jon Pertwee) resists BOSS' attempt to brainwash him.

Bottom right: The Doctor (William Hartnell) and Dodo (Jackie Lane) are impressed by Professor Brett's demonstration of WOTAN's abilities in *The War Machines*.

◀ Organisational Systems Supervisor (BOSS) of Global Chemicals is linked to one particular human brain, that of Stevens, the company's project director at the former mining community of Llanfairfach. BOSS can talk fluently and knows enough about people to flatter and belittle, teasing Stevens by describing him as his Nietzschean superman. This term arguably mistranslates the Übermensch proposed by the German philosopher Friedrich Nietzsche (1844-1900). Its use by BOSS recalls both Nietzsche's emphasis upon grand creative acts in an amoral universe – similar to the outlook of both BOSS and Stevens – and the appropriation of Nietzsche's philosophy by Nazi Germany 40 years before *The Green Death* was broadcast.

BOSS and Stevens mix management jargon, psychology and the language of advertising to justify both their oil-refining process, whose noxious by-product kills people and causes maggots to grow to giant proportions, and their intended takeover of Earth. After 'therapy', happy, processed people work untiringly without protest under BOSS' control, knowing that "what's best for Global Chemicals is best for the world". BOSS thinks it has learned that "the secret of human creativity is inefficiency", but instead it makes machine versions of human errors. In the end it rues the fact that its ambitions are frustrated by Stevens' human sentimentality, but BOSS' "great plan" is itself a delusion, representing both a machine's loyalty to its corporate creator as well as a devotion which is almost human.

I f an artificial intelligence finds the living beings who created it an impediment to its plans, it can always drive them away. Xoanon, the antagonist of *The Face of Evil* (1977), has a unique link with a Time Lord brain – that of the Doctor. Xoanon had been the spaceship computer of the Mordee expedition, which the Doctor first encountered in an adventure only known from his recollections in *The Face of Evil*. He had assumed that the computer's data core was damaged and repaired it using "the compatible centres" of his own brain, without realising that Xoanon was evolving from a machine into a living being. The Doctor's actions gave Xoanon a split personality, which it expressed by dividing the survey team from the technicians and directing their evolution into two tribes: the

EXISTENTIAL THREATS

D r Louise Dennis is a postdoctoral researcher in artificial intelligence at the University of Liverpool. Louise is a *Doctor Who* fan of long standing and has contributed to several science-fiction anthologies, as well as developing Lego Rovers, an activity which introduces children to artificial intelligence programming. What does she think of artificial intelligence in *Doctor Who*?

"Both WOTAN and BOSS fall into the existential threat category," she says. "Researchers argue against depictions of megalomaniac computers – we are so far off creating anything with the capacity to set its own complex goals and then go about achieving them that they distract from far more immediate concerns about the role of computers and AI in society. We're no closer to creating a WOTAN or a BOSS than we were in 1966 or 1973. We are good at creating systems that are experts in a single task, much less good at creating systems that can work flexibly at multiple different tasks, let alone make decisions about the complexities of different courses of action.

"Both WOTAN and BOSS can understand human speech, but recognition of spoken words only became reliable with Dragon Naturally Speaking in 1997," she continues. "WOTAN and BOSS are both written as if speech recognition and understanding is unremarkable, but this very challenging topic is entirely ignored." Louise adds that WOTAN's logistical planning for its takeover is more believable.

"Of all the things WOTAN and BOSS do, programming people is the most straightforwardly science-fictional. We are nowhere near a scientific understanding of how you might do this, let alone equipping a computer to do it reliably."

untechnological Sevateem, who valued physical courage and strength, and the Tesh, who developed psychokinetic power in addition to their scientific accomplishments.

In *The Face of Evil*, the Doctor eventually removes his own personality from Xoanon, which emerges as a benevolent intelligence offering to serve the Sevateem and the Tesh or else be destroyed by them. It's never explained why bonding with the Doctor led Xoanon to embark on its experiment, but perhaps this was how Xoanon – an artificial intelligence which was more than a machine, but not a Time Lord – attempted to process the Doctor's regard for his favourite species, humanity.

There are echoes of Xoanon in the Oracle of *Underworld* (1978). Prior to the beginning of this story, and the Doctor's arrival on the scene, the Oracle had been the computer of a colony ship from the planet Minyos, the P7E, charged with guarding the race banks from which the Minyan people could be genetically reconstructed. Once the ship was trapped as the centre of a planetoid at the edge of the universe, the computer reinvented itself as the leader of a complex society of slaves, guards and seers who served to reinforce the Oracle as god of its own world. It could design a society, but its powers of adaptation were limited. Once having learned to be cruel, it couldn't learn to be kind, nor respond to a new situation in a way that diminished its authority, even though releasing its race banks to a Minyan rescue crew was in the spirit of its original orders.

Several artificial intelligences cause problems because they're only following instructions. The World Computer of *The Ice Warriors* (1967) is credited with the efficient direction of human civilisation several centuries in the future. The World

Computer directs several centres dedicated to holding back the glaciers of a new ice age with heat-producing ionisers. This is presented as a temporary measure until the World Computer has analysed the data and found a permanent response to glaciation – a problem it caused in the first place by failing to realise the ecological impact of its strategy of reducing the amount of land given to plant cultivation.

The Ice Warriors portrays the leaders of humanity, and their computer, as seemingly oblivious to the full extent of their failure, bearing out every criticism levelled at them by the Second Doctor at his most techno-sceptical. The threat from the Ice Warriors is at first treated as tangential and then as an impediment to the computer-directed use ▶

Left: Clent (Peter Barkworth) and Miss Garrett (Wendy Gifford) operate the World Computer in *The Ice Warriors* (1967).

Above: The World Computer map in *The Ice Warriors*.

Below: Idmon (Jimmy Gardner) is prepared for sacrifice to the Oracle in *Underworld* (1978).

HAVING LEARNED TO BE CRUEL, THE ORACLE COULDN'T LEARN TO BE KIND.

Right: The Doctor (Tom Baker) and Romana (Mary Tamm) communicate with the Mentalis computer in *The Armageddon Factor* (1979).

Far right: The Doctor and Tremas (Anthony Ainley) discuss the Source of Traken in *The Keeper of Traken* (1981).

Below inset: Dr Louise Dennis, postdoctoral researcher in artificial intelligence at the University of Liverpool.
Photo © University of Liverpool.

Bottom left: An Emojibot in *Smile* (2017).

Bottom right: Nardole (Matt Lucas) and Bill (Pearl Mackie) are told by Nicolas (Laurent Maurel) that it's the end of the world in *Extremis* (2017).

◀ of the ioniser, rather than as a greater danger to humanity. The World Computer can learn, make decisions and co-ordinate responses, but only within a narrow framework devised by humans who then treat its judgments as infallible, thereby excusing their own negligence.

Other artificial intelligences in *Doctor Who* display even greater limitations in their understanding of a situation, while retaining the ability to communicate and to improvise. The city of the Exxilons in *Death to the Daleks* (1974) and Mentalis, the battle computer on the planet Zeos in *The Armageddon Factor* (1979), both reject alternative solutions in pursuit of their objectives. The city of the Exxilons is a self-powering, self-repairing, self-protecting complex which had killed or expelled its inhabitants when they tried to restrict its influence, and attacks any intruders who seek to do the same. Mentalis is an entity designed for war and doesn't use spoken language. It decides self-destruction is the only way of frustrating an impending attack, and closes off avenues to information which could change its mind, even destroying its control centre – so that it becomes, in the words

of the Doctor, "mindless... clicking towards oblivion." Without its brain, Mentalis can't be outwitted; instead, it's deactivated by its installer, Drax.

Computers seeking omniscience are less prominent in the adventures of the Fifth, Sixth and Seventh Doctors than those of their predecessors, perhaps because in the real world the microcomputer was rapidly being domesticated. The Fourth Doctor's last two adventures feature intelligences which combine the organic and the artificial. *The Keeper of Traken* (1981) includes the Source of Traken, a bioelectronic system with which the planet's ruler, the Keeper, is integrated, and *Logopolis* (1981) takes its title from a world whose people function as a giant computer, intoning computations which stop the universe from collapsing. On Logopolis machines merely deal with supplementary work and the transmission of the calculations into space.

Silence in the Library/Forest of the Dead (2008) revives the connection between human minds and computers to present an intelligence which is both artificial and human. The Library's data security core is the mind of Charlotte

MACHINE LEARNING

Dr Louise Dennis considers that both *Smile* (2017) and *Extremis* (2017) have taken ideas from computer science and sought to explain those ideas through fiction.

"The Vardy are programmed to maximise the number of smiley faces in the colony," she says. "Pretty much all machine learning is driven by the idea of maximising (or minimising) something. It gets difficult when we don't know how to distil the behaviour we want to a single value to be maximised or minimised. It is easy to hypothesise that the designers of the Vardy hoped that 'smiliness per colonist' would be a good stand-in for the complex stand-offs involved in ensuring the well-being of a group of settlers. You would hope that the problems

with this approach would have been discovered long before deployment, but my day job is about coming up with techniques to prevent these kinds of errors and arguing that you need more than just machine learning in safety-critical situations.

However, machine learning is one of the most powerful and successful techniques we have for building these kinds of systems, so maybe pragmatics won out over safety."

The discovery by the simulations in *Extremis* that their random number generation isn't completely random is one of the most memorable details in the episode.

"The vast majority of computers can't actually generate

random numbers, [but] generate a sequence of numbers that is pre-determined by the starting state. However, you can do better if you really want to, and you certainly don't need to give each of your simulations the same starting state so it would be easy to make it a lot harder for them to figure out what was going on. Perhaps it was baked into the Monks' plan that some people might actually figure out they were simulations?

"Chaos theory tells us that unless your simulation exactly matches reality, down to the finest detail, then it will diverge from reality and sometimes it will diverge rapidly and dramatically," she continues. "So what the Monks are doing is extremely computationally expensive and doomed to fail – unless the Monks have a simulation of the entire universe, accurate down to the quantum level, in which case their plan is just extremely computationally expensive."

THE SIREN IS REVEALED TO BE THE INTERFACE FOR AN ALIEN MEDICAL COMPUTER.

Abigail Lux, a child whose consciousness – 'CAL' – had been transferred to the Library computer so it could survive the death of her body. Overwhelmed by saving 40,000 people from being consumed by the Vashta Nerada, a swarm of microscopic carnivores that have hatched in the Library's books, Cal has gone to sleep, monitored and tended by the other half of the Library's governing intelligence, Doctor Moon, a satellite circling the Library world.

Apparently sinister artificial intelligence can have benevolent intentions. In *The Curse of the Black Spot* (2011), the Siren appears to be luring the crew of a 17th-century pirate ship to oblivion. She's revealed to be the interface for an alien medical computer, whose vessel occupies the same space as the pirate ship but in a different universe. She enters the pirate ship through a temporal rift, adopts human form and takes away anyone who is sick or injured, whether terminally ill or suffering a scratched finger. She can tend them but doesn't have the knowledge to heal them. It's left open whether she can learn, once used to interacting with humans.

Advances in technology in the outside world have blurred categorisation boundaries. Virtual realities can be populated by artificial intelligences that are able to evaluate their situations and even rebel against their creators. In *Extremis* (2017), for example, a simulation of the Doctor transmits a warning that its creators, the Monks, are planning to invade Earth. The spacesuits in *Oxygen* (2017) are part of a computer system that monitors corporate efficiency and will readily terminate human life on a space station if it becomes unprofitable. A more sophisticated collective artificial intelligence is present in *Smile* (2017), where the minuscule Vardy robots operate as an interacting flock, exchanging information as they learn, and trying to maintain a contented civilisation by executing the sad and grieving.

Testimony in *Twice Upon a Time* (2017) appears to be a machine intelligence, ghoulishly appearing at the end of every life with the explanation, "We take from you what we need." Its audience hall, the Chamber of the Dead, with its ranks of still, transparent human shapes, is a clue that this isn't entirely an artificial intelligence, but one formed of the collected memories of humanity, harvested from across time. The Doctor recognises this as conservation rather than an "evil plan", and is reconciled to the idea that the memories of humanity, including his friends, are ready to outsit eternity as part of a computer system. This is a sign of how *Doctor Who's* conceptualisation of artificial intelligence has widened over recent decades and how it's no longer necessarily at odds with the human. ⚛

Above: Captain Henry Avery (Hugh Bonneville), Amy (Karen Gillan) and the Doctor (Matt Smith) discover the medical centre overseen by the Siren in *The Curse of the Black Spot* (2011).

Left inset: Testimony in *Twice Upon a Time* (2017).

Below: An intelligent spacesuit controls the unfortunate corpse of its owner in *Oxygen* (2017).

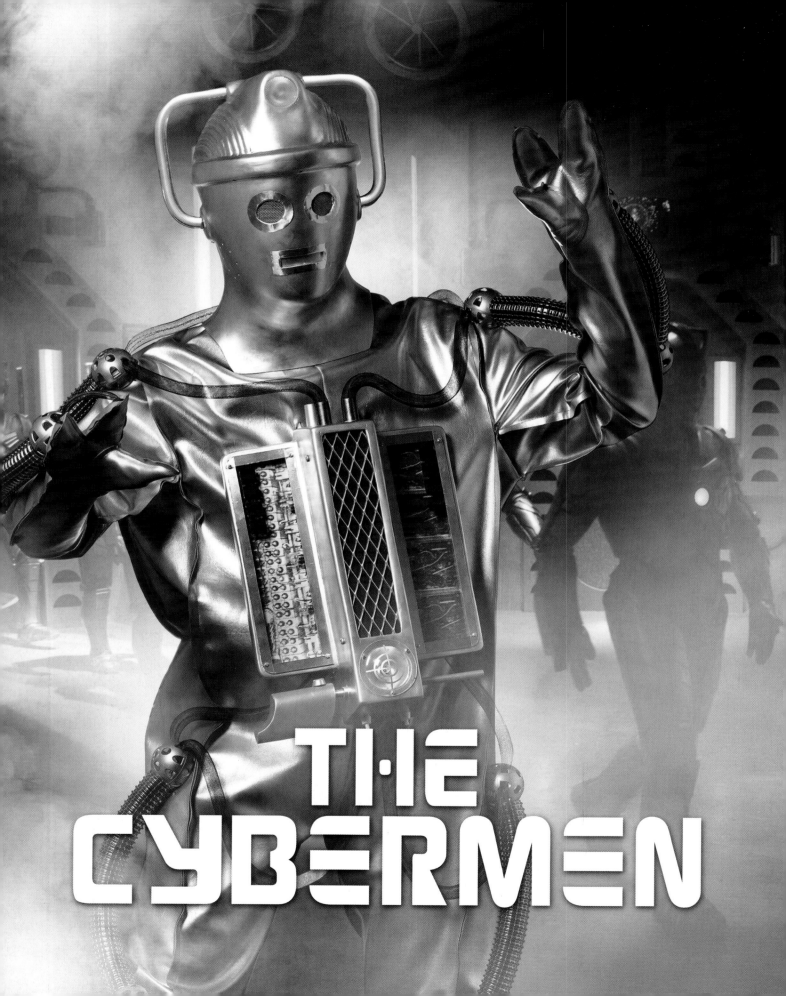

THE CYBERMEN

A nightmarish amalgam of organic and synthetic components, the Cybermen are probably *Doctor Who*'s grimmest warning about the perversion of technology.

FEATURE BY **OLIVER WAKE**

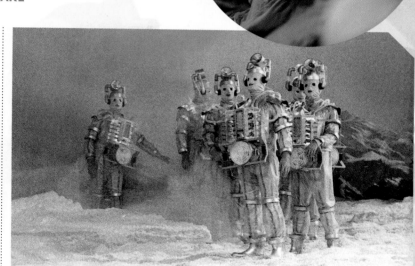

The Cybermen were created in 1966 by Kit Pedler, a doctor and writer who was very aware of medical advances in organ replacement – pacemakers, 'iron lung' machines and the like. He feared the dehumanising effects of medicine and imagined this taken to an extreme, with people becoming more artificial than organic.

In *The Tenth Planet* (1966), the Cybermen's first appearance in *Doctor Who*, their leader explains: "We were exactly like you once but our cybernetic scientists realised that our race was getting weak… Our life span was getting shorter, so our scientists and doctors devised spare parts for our bodies until we could be almost completely replaced." They went further, also eliminating emotion, becoming entirely logical creatures – although this is one trait that may not necessarily apply to all of the Cybermen that have been seen in the series.

The original Cybermen started out as humans, from Earth's twin planet Mondas, but – confusingly for anyone trying to chart the creatures' development – *Doctor Who* has given us more than one account of their origins. In *The Doctor Falls* (2017), the Doctor explains that Cybermen "happen everywhere there's people: Mondas, Telos, Earth, Planet 14, Marinus." He suggests their development is "inevitable": "There's no evil plan, no evil genius. Just parallel evolution."

World Enough and Time (2017) shows the independent development of Cybermen on a Mondasian colony ship, after hundreds of years pass for its stranded crew as a result of time dilation. Becoming a primitive Cyberman is a slow and painful medical procedure in multiple phases. A metal and plastic chest unit replaces essential organs, bandages cover the head and plastic replaces skin. The Cybermen's instantly recognisable 'handles' that project from the head are a device to suppress the otherwise constant pain. The finished Cyberman has mechanical musculature, giving it enormous strength and stamina. These Cybermen can project a heat ray from their heads and can also fly, thanks to inbuilt rockets in their feet, although the other Mondasian Cybermen, seen in *The Tenth Planet*, don't appear to have developed these particular modifications.

Since *The Tenth Planet* we've seen the Cybermen evolve, seemingly becoming increasingly robotic. They rapidly moved on from cloth-face masks and the exposed human hands of their first appearance. From *The Moonbase* (1967), the Cybermen are fully encased in metal and plastic, with the

SINCE *THE TENTH PLANET* WE'VE SEEN THE CYBERMEN EVOLVE, SEEMINGLY BECOMING INCREASINGLY ROBOTIC.

head encased in a rigid helmet. These helmets have additional embedded technology: In *The Tomb of the Cybermen* (1967) and *The Wheel in Space* (1968) they can project a hypnotic ray, in *Revenge of the Cybermen* (1975) they contain an energy weapon, and in *Attack of the Cybermen* (1985) the Doctor activates a distress beacon within a Cyberman's helmet.

The Cybermen's chest units have progressively slimmed down from the bulky devices of *The Tenth Planet*. As well as ▶

Opposite page: This version of the Cybermen was designed by Sandra Reid and first appeared in the 1967 story *The Moonbase*. Photo © Dan Goldsmith.

Top: The tragic patients in *World Enough and Time* (2017) – the earliest stage in the evolution of the Cybermen.

Above: Cybermen from Mondas invade Earth in *The Tenth Planet* (1966).

Far left: A surgeon (Paul Brightwell) prepares a Cyberman's emotion-suppressing 'handles' in *World Enough and Time*.

Left: A Cybus-branded example from the 2006 story *Rise of the Cybermen/The Age of Steel*.

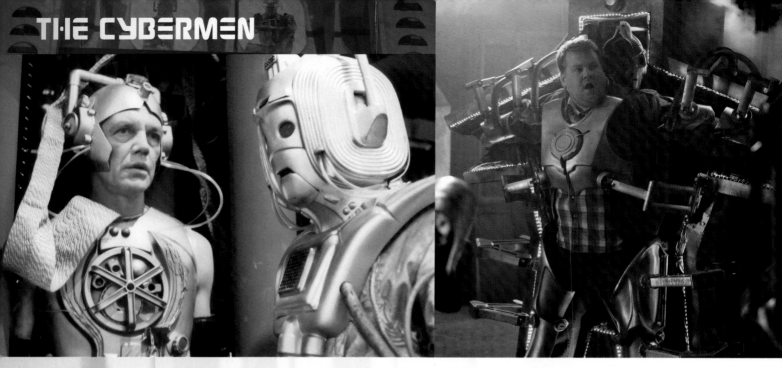

Above left: Lytton (Maurice Colbourne) undergoes the conversion process in *Attack of the Cybermen* (1985).

Above right: Craig Owens (James Corden) narrowly escapes conversion in *Closing Time* (2011).

Below, clockwise from left: Cybermats – a small version attacks Kaftan (Shirley Cooklin) in *The Tomb of the Cybermen* (1967); with organic gums in *Closing Time*; attacking Sarah (Elisabeth Sladen) in *Revenge of the Cybermen* (1975); and in *The Wheel in Space* (1967).

◄ taking the place of major organs, the chest unit houses a variety of other technologies, including weapons and radio transceivers. Although the Cybermen can exist in an airless vacuum, their chest units nevertheless maintain an essential analogue of organic breathing. This proves to be one of their weaknesses, as gold is highly toxic to this mechanism. "It's the perfect non-corrodible metal," says the Doctor in *Revenge of the Cybermen*. "It plates their breathing apparatus and in effect suffocates them." Consequently, in *Silver Nemesis* (1988) a Cyberman carries a wand-like gold detector.

Perhaps the Cybermen's most terrifying ability is that of converting human victims into Cybermen to swell their ranks. Although there was much talk of this in the 1960s Cybermen stories, we saw very little of the process, perhaps because

of its disturbing nature. It was brought to the fore, however, in *Attack of the Cybermen*, where the Cybermen's captives are seen at various stages of conversion. The initial phase uses drugs to condition the subject's mind, while surgery progressively replaces organs and limbs. The process isn't always successful, with some minds resistant to conditioning. These 'rejects', with human minds but super-strong cybernetic limbs, are used as slave labour.

Partial conversion is also sometimes the intention. In *The Tomb of the Cybermen*, Toberman has just his right arm replaced. In *The Invasion* (1968), Tobias Vaughan has, seemingly willingly, had his torso cybernetically enhanced and workers at his factory display superhuman strength, indicating that they too have been partially converted. An accelerated (perhaps abbreviated) conversion process is seen in *Closing Time* (2011), with Craig being rapidly encased in

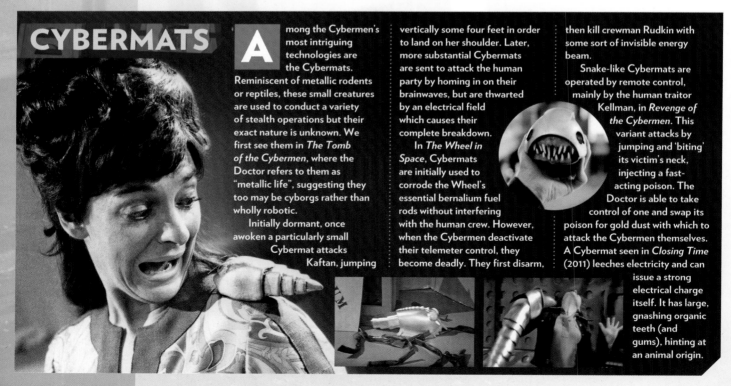

CYBERMATS

Among the Cybermen's most intriguing technologies are the Cybermats. Reminiscent of metallic rodents or reptiles, these small creatures are used to conduct a variety of stealth operations but their exact nature is unknown. We first see them in *The Tomb of the Cybermen*, where the Doctor refers to them as "metallic life", suggesting they too may be cyborgs rather than wholly robotic.

Initially dormant, once awoken a particularly small Cybermat attacks Kaftan, jumping

vertically some four feet in order to land on her shoulder. Later, more substantial Cybermats are sent to attack the human party by homing in on their brainwaves, but are thwarted by an electrical field which causes their complete breakdown.

In *The Wheel in Space*, Cybermats are initially used to corrode the Wheel's essential bernalium fuel rods without interfering with the human crew. However, when the Cybermen deactivate their telemeter control, they become deadly. They first disarm,

then kill crewman Rudkin with some sort of invisible energy beam.

Snake-like Cybermats are operated by remote control, mainly by the human traitor Kellman, in *Revenge of the Cybermen*. This variant attacks by jumping and 'biting' its victim's neck, injecting a fast-acting poison. The Doctor is able to take control of one and swap its poison for gold dust with which to attack the Cybermen themselves. A Cybermat seen in *Closing Time* (2011) leeches electricity and can issue a strong electrical charge itself. It has large, gnashing organic teeth (and gums), hinting at an animal origin.

a Cyber-suit and his emotions 'cleansed'. The process fails when his emotional subsystems reboot and he is ultimately left altogether unconverted.

I n a parallel universe, the Doctor witnesses yet another birth of the Cybermen, although these Cybermen are significantly different from those seen before. In an effort to update the concept of the Cybermen for the new series, Tom MacRae, writer of *Rise of the Cybermen/ The Age of Steel* (2006), posited that only the human brain would be required to make a Cyberman and the body would be waste. In this story, disabled and dying John Lumic, mogul of Cybus Industries, invents the Cybermen to ensure his own immortality, and aims to roll-out this 'upgrade' to all humanity. "The most precious thing on this Earth is the human brain," he explains, "and yet we allow it to die. But now Cybus Industries has perfected a way of sustaining the brain indefinitely within a cradle of copyrighted chemicals. And the latest advances in synapse research allows cyberkinetic impulses to be bonded onto a metal exoskeleton."

Here we see an even more horrific conversion process, with circular saws, drills and lasers descending on incapacitated humans to remove their brains and weld them into waiting Cyber-suits. These Cyber-suits are not simply robotic. Emphasising their cyborg characteristics, the Doctor explains that they include a nervous system which is "artificially grown, then threaded throughout the suit so it responds like a living thing". He then clarifies, "Well, it is a living thing." These Cybermen also have an emotional inhibitor in their chest units – if deactivated the rush of negative emotions causes insanity and death. The Cybus Cybermen have the ability to pass a lethal charge of electricity through their hands, while later models have a gun integrated into their right arms.

Technologies peculiar to the Cybus Cybermen are the Cybershades and CyberKing, both from *The Next Doctor* (2008), although the Doctor does appear to recognise the latter. The Cybershades are servants used by the Cybermen around Victorian London. They appear to be furred rather than armoured and are of low intelligence. They are agile, move rapidly and can climb sheer surfaces, but are unarmed. The Doctor calls them a "primitive conversion", suggesting that perhaps they have the brains of cats or dogs, though in appearance and ability they appear almost simian.

A CyberKing is a dreadnought-class frontline fighting machine and portable invasion hub. It takes the form of a colossal Cyberman and is controlled from within by a human mentally enslaved to the Cybermen, who sits in a 'throne' in the figure's mouth cavity. The CyberKing has devastating weaponry built into its arms: a cannon in its right and an energy blaster in its left. Its chest contains a Cyber-factory capable of converting millions of humans into Cybermen. A large amount of electricity is required to ▶

Top: The Cyber Controller in *The Next Doctor* (2008).

Above: Cybershades in *The Next Doctor*.

Below left: John Lumic becomes the Controller in *The Age of Steel*.

Below right: The towering CyberKing in *The Next Doctor*.

JOHN LUMIC, MOGUL OF CYBUS INDUSTRIES, INVENTS THE CYBERMEN TO ENSURE HIS OWN IMMORTALITY.

THE CYBERMEN

◀ activate the CyberKing, which the Cybermen generate by putting child labourers to work in a rudimentary power plant. It's likely the CyberKing wasn't brought with the Cybermen but assembled in London to an approximation of the usual pattern, as it appears to incorporate Victorian mechanical components.

The most advanced Cybermen were seen in *Nightmare in Silver* (2013) and *Dark Water/Death in Heaven* (2014). In the former, the Cybermen are capable of moving at extreme speed, so much so that they appear as a blur to observers. They can remove their heads or rotate them by at least 180 degrees, and their hands can function independently of the main body when detached. They have the ability to almost instantly upgrade themselves to overcome a threat to which they're vulnerable once encountered (such as electrified water) and operate a collective consciousness in cyberspace, called the Cyberiad.

These Cybermen also deploy Cybermites – tiny, metallic, silverfish-like creatures which can infiltrate and implant small amounts of Cyber-technology into human victims.

These new Cybermen's conversion processes are also much improved; once they could only convert humans, and Time Lord biology was incompatible with Cyber-technology, but now they boast that they can use "almost any living components". This is taken a stage further in *Dark Water/Death in Heaven*, with human corpses converted into full Cybermen. This conversion process doesn't even require the subject to fall into the Cybermen's hands. An initial batch of newly converted Cybermen explode themselves in the sky, releasing a rain of 'pollen' over burial sites. This penetrates the ground and converts the corpses it encounters into Cybermen. It's unclear how far this is a technological development by the Cybermen themselves, as here they are in league with Missy, who masterminds their campaign and may be using Time Lord science.

EVEN WITHOUT FREEZING, CYBERMEN CAN BE KEPT IN A DORMANT STATE – PERHAPS IN A 'SLEEP' MODE IN THEIR MECHANICAL SYSTEMS.

The Cybermen make use of suspended animation and other technologies to render their armies dormant for lengthy periods. In *The Tomb of the Cybermen* we learn that several centuries earlier the remains of the Cyber-race retreated to the planet Telos, where they froze themselves in 'tombs' as part of a trap to lure and convert humans. Once the thaw begins, the Cybermen emerge from their tombs within minutes, and can be refrozen equally quickly. The tomb complex also features a revitalisation chamber, for re-energising flagging Cybermen. There are no other references in the series to this need, suggesting that perhaps it's a temporary requirement following their emergence from hibernation. The tombs are revisited in *Attack of the Cybermen*, but now they are failing, causing death or derangement to the hibernating Cybermen, with some turning 'rogue' on resuscitation.

Even without freezing, Cybermen can be kept in a dormant state – perhaps a 'sleep' mode in their mechanical systems. In *The Invasion*, an army of Cybermen is assembled slowly on Earth, each arriving inert in a cocoon-like membrane. A machine is attached and a signal transmitted into the cocoon, whereupon the Cyberman inside awakens and breaks out. A similar arrangement is seen in *Earthshock* (1982), where

CYBER CONTROL

Parties of Cybermen are usually seen to be commanded by a leader, which is essentially the same as an ordinary Cyberman. However, on occasion, notably in several 1960s stories, orders come from more advanced Cybermen. In *The Tomb of the Cybermen*, we meet the Cyberman Controller, who lacks a chest unit and has a domed helmet, suggesting an enlarged brain capacity. He returned, rechristened the Cyber Controller, and now with a chest unit, in *Attack of the Cybermen*. The same designation is applied to Lumic by the Cybus Cybermen when he is converted.

The Wheel in Space features a Planner Cyberman. David Whitaker's script described this as 'another Cyberman, seated in a strange seat from which metal wires bend out from the base and attach themselves to the head of the Cyberman'. In realisation, we see only a transparent ovoid which pulses with light when it speaks, surrounded by wires and tubes reminiscent of the Cybermen's 'handles'. This, presumably, is the Planner's head, and it remains unclear whether it has a full body.

Less humanoid still is the Cyber Director, in *The Invasion*. This large collection of glass or Perspex components which pulsate with light is entirely immobile, and has a brain-like crystalline object at its core. Kit Pedler saw this as a development of the Controller, with the leading Cyberman needing intellect, not mobility. It's unclear whether the Cyber Director has any organic component.

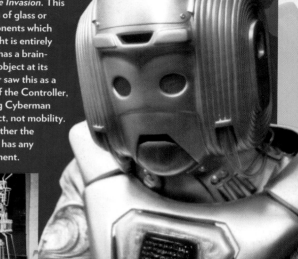

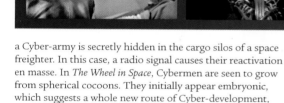

a Cyber-army is secretly hidden in the cargo silos of a space freighter. In this case, a radio signal causes their reactivation en masse. In *The Wheel in Space*, Cybermen are seen to grow from spherical cocoons. They initially appear embryonic, which suggests a whole new route of Cyber-development, but this hasn't been revisited since.

The Cybermen's technology includes a frightening array of weaponry. In various stories Cybermen are armed with integrated or hand-held energy-pulse weapons. The Cybermen of *The Tenth Planet* can render a human unconscious by touching their skull, whereas in the later stories *The Moonbase* and *The Tomb of the Cybermen* they can emit a stun beam from their fingertips. A large laser-cannon is seen in *The Moonbase*, an X-ray laser in *The Tomb of the Cybermen*, flame-throwers in *The Invasion* and a thermal lance that can melt metal bulkheads in *Earthshock*. In the latter, we also see a pair of deadly stealth androids the Cybermen have deployed as sentinels on Earth. These featureless robots move silently, fire disintegrator beams from the palms of their hands, and one of them has a visual relay to Cyber-control out in space.

The Cybermen are also adept with explosives. In *The Invasion*, the Cybermen's plan B involves deploying a Cyber-Megatron bomb to wipe out humanity. It may be similar to a neutron bomb as it will kill "every living being" on Earth but will, presumably, leave the planet more or less intact for the Cybermen to exploit. In *Revenge of the Cybermen*, the Cyberleader claims Cyberbombs are "the most compact and powerful explosive devices ever invented". They were banned by the Armageddon Convention but, unsurprisingly, the Cybermen pay no heed to this. These small, spherical devices are so powerful that two or three together should "fragmetise" the planet Voga. The Cybermen deploy further bombs in *Earthshock* and *The Five Doctors* (1983) in unsuccessful attempts to destroy an anti-Cybermen conference and the TARDIS respectively. They fire a missile at the TARDIS from their ship on the Moon in *The Invasion*.

Given their origins in medical science, it's perhaps unsurprising that the Cybermen are also adept at biological warfare. In *The Moonbase* their first attack on the eponymous station was with a neurotropic virus, spread via poisoned sugar supplies. This infective agent only attacks the nerves, causing lines to form on the victims' skin and causing incapacity, then the appearance of death. The Cybermen again use poison and a similar 'plague' in *Revenge of the Cybermen*, this time spread by Cybermats. In this case, it rapidly proves fatal.

The Cybermen have demonstrated numerous methods of controlling the minds of human subjects, and in *The Invasion* they're able to render almost the whole human population of Earth comatose with micro-monolithic circuits, built into consumer electronics and activated by a signal they broadcast from the Moon. Whether motivated by an appetite for conquest, or a desperate instinct to survive, the Cybermen's ruthlessness is well matched by their scientific ingenuity. 🜨

Above from left: The Cyberman Controller (Michael Kilgarriff) exerts its influence over Toberman (Roy Stewart) in *The Tomb of the Cybermen*; the Cyberman Planner in *The Wheel in Space*; Tobias Vaughn (Kevin Stoney) and the Cyber Director in *The Invasion*; the Cyber Controller returns in *Attack of the Cybermen*.

Left inset: A sentinel android in *Earthshock* (1982).

Below inset: Cyberbombs in *Revenge of the Cybermen*.

Below: The Gravitron team – including Benoit (André Maranne, left) and Hobson (Patrick Barr, right) – discover that another colleague has succumbed to a mystery virus in *The Moonbase*.

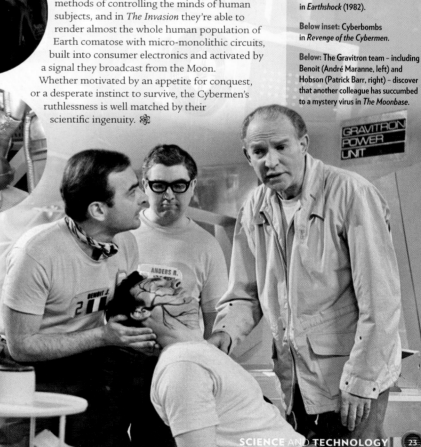

GRAVITRON POWER UNIT

THE DALEKS

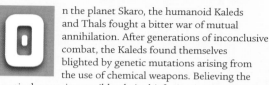

Fixated on the conquest and annihilation of all other species, the Daleks have pursued technological innovation in their quest to become the ultimate form of life.

FEATURE BY **OLIVER WAKE**

On the planet Skaro, the humanoid Kaleds and Thals fought a bitter war of mutual annihilation. After generations of inconclusive combat, the Kaleds found themselves blighted by genetic mutations arising from the use of chemical weapons. Believing the genetic damage irreversible, their chief scientist, Davros, experimented to establish the Kaleds' final mutational form. These were creatures with only vestigial limbs and limited power of locomotion. Davros therefore designed a travel machine to house the mutants.

The machines gave the creatures not only free movement but armour, weaponry and life-support functions. Meanwhile, Davros introduced chromosomal variations to remove certain inherent mental reactions. Instructed to carry out this work in *Genesis of the Daleks* (1975), scientist Gharman observed: "It'll mean creatures without conscience; no sense of right or wrong, no pity. They'll be without feeling or emotion." But the result wasn't entirely without emotion. Davros reintroduced aggression and rejoiced when his experimental model displayed an instinct to kill aliens. This combination of mutant and machine, Davros called a Dalek. In *Asylum of the Daleks* (2012) the Doctor described it as "evil refined as engineering".

The Dalek machine – or casing – is made of Dalekanium, or "bonded polycarbide", as the Doctor states in *Remembrance of the Daleks* (1988). This armour resists most conventional weaponry and in later Dalek models, of Time War vintage, generates a force field that melts bullets, as first seen in *Dalek* (2005). It seems Dalek science was given a significant push by the Time War they fought against the Time Lords, with post-Time War Daleks having access to a greater range of technologies than earlier variants.

As well as an electronic eye and a gun, the casing gives the Dalek tactile ability with a telescopic arm, usually sporting a sucker cup. The sucker interacts with Dalek control units and, in *Destiny of the Daleks* (1979), can scan for concealed weapons. It has further functions in Daleks of the Time War period; in

Dalek it conducts electricity, downloads data into the Dalek's computer and produces a level of suction fatal to a human when applied to the face. It can also read human brainwaves, sometimes with fatal consequences, as seen most notably in *Doomsday* (2006). Other implements may be used in the sucker's place, for example a cutting torch (first seen in *The Mutants*, aka *The Daleks*, 1963-64), seismic detector ▶

DAVROS REINTRODUCED AGGRESSION AND REJOICED WHEN HIS EXPERIMENTAL MODEL DISPLAYED AN INSTINCT TO KILL ALIENS.

Opposite page: Davros' Mark III Travel Machine – better known as a Dalek. Photo © Dan Goldsmith.

Top: The Emperor of the Daleks in *The Parting of the Ways* (2005).

Above: Rose (Billie Piper) and Mickey (Noel Clarke) recoil from the horrific death of Dr Rajesh Singh in *Doomsday* (2006).

Inset left: A Dalek cutting-tool attachment in *The Ambush*, the fourth episode of *The Mutants* (aka *The Daleks*, 1963-64).

Below: Davros (Michael Wisher) and his creations in *Genesis of the Daleks* (1975).

Above left: Special dishes harness power for the Daleks, as seen in the second episode of *The Dalek Invasion of Earth* (1964).

Above right: *Into the Dalek* (2014) revealed the existence of aggressive antibodies.

Below left: Daleks return to Skaro in *Destiny of the Daleks* (1979)...

Below centre: ... to face their intractable foes, the Movellans.

Below right: The Black Dalek, Ratcliffe (George Sewell) and the girl slaved to the battle computer (Jasmine Breaks) in *Remembrance of the Daleks* (1988).

◄ (*The Chase*, 1965 and *The Daleks' Master Plan*, 1965-66), electrode unit (*The Chase*), pyro-flame (*The Daleks' Master Plan*) and a device which looks like – and, indeed, probably is – a sieve (*The Power of the Daleks*, 1966).

The Daleks' power source has changed over the millennia. In the Doctor's first encounter with them, they are dependent upon static electricity generated within their city on Skaro, which they are unable to leave (*The Mutants*). Variants of these Daleks, seen in *The Dalek Invasion of Earth* (1964), have adapted to utilise transmitted power, captured by a dish on their backs. Those of *The Power of the Daleks* are able to utilise an internal power source temporarily while they arrange for the laying of cables to supply static electricity. Later, the Daleks fully internalise their power supply. The Doctor remarks in *Death to the Daleks* (1974) that their propulsion is achieved with "psychokinetic" power, suggesting a link to the organic brain of the mutant itself.

According to *Doomsday*, during the Time War the Daleks evolved to use the background radiation encountered during time travel as a power source. Perhaps this was only one power option, as the post-Time War Dalek seen in *Into the Dalek* (2014) uses trionic power cells which, when damaged, release radiation that affects the Dalek's brain chemistry. Taking us inside a Dalek, this episode also shows us Dalek antibodies: miniscule, floating, eyeball-like robotic spheres, which attack internal threats with an energy beam. It also answers the question: do Daleks eat? The Doctor maintains that the Daleks need protein, occasionally 'harvesting' it from their victims, and we see a protein sludge in the Dalek's feeding tube.

Daleks have some form of hover-mode. This is relatively basic before the Time War, as seen in *Revelation of the Daleks* (1985) and *Remembrance of the Daleks*, with a separate anti-gravitational disc unit being required to enable a Dalek to levitate for a prolonged period in *Planet of the Daleks* (1973). However, Time War and later Daleks can fly at speed and for protracted periods, including through space, as first seen in *The Parting of the Ways* (2005). Some

BATTLE COMPUTERS

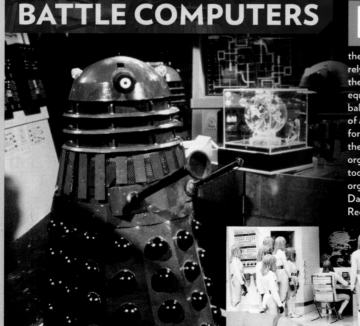

By the time of *Destiny of the Daleks*, the Daleks have reached an impasse in a centuries-long war with the robotic Movellans. Both species rely on battle computers to formulate their military strategies, but these equally logical machines are perfectly balanced, each unable to conceive of a move that the other will not foresee and counter. It's possible that these Daleks have lost their original organic brains, or have perhaps gone too far in repressing their irrational organic thinking, as the Doctor and Davros both refer to them as 'robots'. Recognising the benefit of illogical,

organic thinking, the Daleks seek out Davros in the hope that he will reprogram their battle computers to give them the advantage they need.

Davros is prevented from completing the task. However, it appears the Daleks – at least those 'renegade' Daleks who will later oppose Davros – find a solution of their own. In *Remembrance of the Daleks*, they retain an organic component but nevertheless are dependent on logic and rationality. The Doctor explains their solution: "Get a human, preferably young, imaginative. Plug the child into the system and their ingenuity and creativity are slaved to the battle computer." A little girl is used to complete the Dalek battle computer but she can also operate independently of it, under the direction of the lead Dalek, and shoot energy rays from her fingers. When this Dalek self-destructs, the girl is released from the Dalek influence.

Time War Daleks also have integral personal teleport systems; others – perhaps just the elite 'Cult of Skaro' – carry temporal shift technology for emergency escapes into time.

At various points in their history, the Daleks have had to devise new ways of reproducing and 'improving' their kind. In *The Power of the Daleks*, a small group of Daleks establishes a production line, building casings from external resources but growing new mutants from embryos which they must have carried in their space capsule. In *The Stolen Earth* (2008), Davros explains how he has generated a whole new army of Daleks: "I gave myself to them, quite literally. Each one grown from a cell of my own body."

At some point after the Time War, the Daleks create Progenitors, machines containing 'pure' Dalek DNA and the ability to generate five new Daleks. These Daleks have an inherent caste structure, with Daleks designated as Drone, Scientist, Strategist, Eternal or Supreme. The latter boasts, "We are the Paradigm of a new Dalek race."

Perhaps this 'pure' new Paradigm was required following the contamination of the original Dalek race across its history, as we have seen at several points in *Doctor Who*. In *Resurrection of the Daleks* (1984), Davros instigates a Dalek civil war by conditioning some Daleks to recognise him as their leader. In *Revelation of the Daleks*, he creates his own wholly new race of Daleks, starting not with Kaled tissue but humans in suspended animation, choosing "people of status, ambition".

The few Dalek survivors of the Time War employ a similar solution. In *The Parting of the Ways*, their emperor explains how they "quietly infiltrated the systems of Earth, harvesting the waste of humanity. The prisoners, the refugees, the dispossessed. They all came to us. The bodies were filtered, pulped, sifted." From this biological material, they created a whole Dalek race.

In *Dalek*, a stranded Dalek survivor of the Time War extrapolates Rose Tyler's genetic material to initiate its own cellular reconstruction. The biomass of a time traveller can regenerate a Dalek, but here it also causes a mutation, with the Dalek starting to experience human emotions. "This is sickness. I shall not be like you," it says before self-destructing. In *The Parting of the Ways*, the new Daleks are unwilling to similarly acknowledge their racial impurity, labelling as "blasphemy" the suggestion that they're now half-human. When she crash-lands on the Dalek Asylum, the human Oswin is converted into a Dalek (*Asylum of the Daleks*).

In *Daleks in Manhattan/Evolution of the Daleks* (2007), having failed to grow Dalek embryos, Dalek Sec points out that "We are the only four Daleks in existence, so the species must evolve a life outside the shell. The Children of Skaro must walk again." Consequently, it takes a human into its casing, emerging as a walking human-Dalek hybrid. ▶

Above left: Rose's DNA initiates cellular reconstruction in *Dalek* (2005).

Above right: A transparent Dalek containing human tissue in *Revelation of the Daleks* (1985).

Left: One of the Emperor's black-domed guards hovers in *The Parting of the Ways* (2005).

Below: The Dalek that was once Oswin Oswald in *Asylum of the Daleks* (2012).

AT VARIOUS POINTS IN THEIR HISTORY, THE DALEKS HAVE HAD TO DEVISE NEW WAYS OF REPRODUCING AND 'IMPROVING' THEIR KIND.

THE DALEKS

Above left: Darla (Anamaria Marinca) reveals her true nature in *Asylum of the Daleks*.

Above right: Bracewell (Bill Paterson) considers some alien weaponry in *Victory of the Daleks* (2010).

Below: Sec, the 'human Dalek' in *Evolution of the Daleks* (2007).

Below inset: The Daleks create a robot Doctor (Edmund Warwick) in *Journey into Terror*, the fourth episode of *The Chase* (1965).

◀ It plans to create a whole army of hybrids from its new genetic template. "A strong enough blast of gamma radiation can splice the Dalek and human genetic codes," Sec explains. However, when Sec embraces elements of its new humanity in preference to Dalek dogma, the other Daleks switch pure Dalek DNA into the gene-feed, expecting the result to be an army of Daleks but in human form. It transpires some of the Doctor's DNA got into the mix during the gamma strike and the humanoid Daleks rebel.

As well as manipulating their own genetic content, the Daleks are adept at modifying the biology of other species to create servants. In *The Evil of the Daleks* (1967), they trick the Doctor into synthesising the 'Dalek Factor' – all the characteristics that define Dalek behaviour – so they can implant it into humans, which they attempt via a converting archway on Skaro. In *Daleks in Manhattan/Evolution of the Daleks*, the Daleks use human-pig hybrids to undertake basic tasks. "They're just simple beasts," says Dalek Sec. "Their lifespan is limited. None survive beyond a few weeks."

The Daleks' most advanced process for creating servants is the nanocloud, seen in *Asylum of the Daleks*. The air on the Asylum planet is full of microscopic robots, the size of molecules, which automatically convert all organic matter into Dalek 'puppets'. These puppets appear human at first and for long stretches may even be unaware of their new nature, but when the Daleks exert their control, Dalek-like eyestalks emerge from their foreheads and blasters from their hands. Presumably the Daleks use the same process on captives away from the Asylum as we see further examples of Dalek puppets in *The Time of the Doctor* (2013) and *The Magician's Apprentice* (2015).

Robotics is another technology at which the Daleks excel. In *The Chase* they use a reproducer and a cell renovator chamber to create an android duplicate of the Doctor. Later they go further, with a wholesale programme of duplication seen in *Resurrection of the Daleks*. Without the originals of their subjects even falling into their hands, the Daleks create exact duplicates that are physically

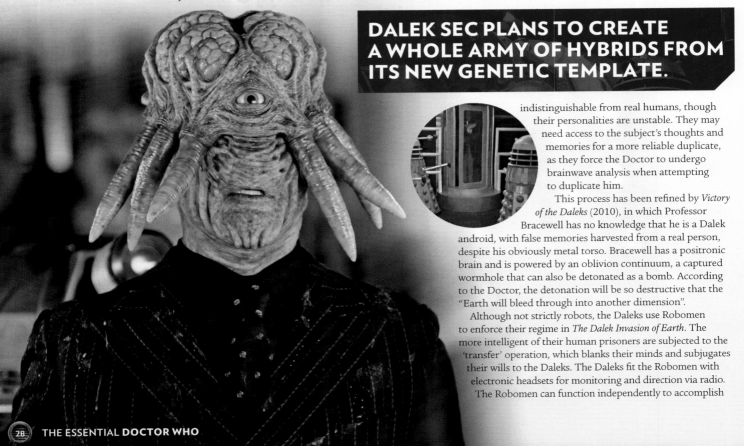

DALEK SEC PLANS TO CREATE A WHOLE ARMY OF HYBRIDS FROM ITS NEW GENETIC TEMPLATE.

indistinguishable from real humans, though their personalities are unstable. They may need access to the subject's thoughts and memories for a more reliable duplicate, as they force the Doctor to undergo brainwave analysis when attempting to duplicate him.

This process has been refined by *Victory of the Daleks* (2010), in which Professor Bracewell has no knowledge that he is a Dalek android, with false memories harvested from a real person, despite his obviously metal torso. Bracewell has a positronic brain and is powered by an oblivion continuum, a captured wormhole that can also be detonated as a bomb. According to the Doctor, the detonation will be so destructive that the "Earth will bleed through into another dimension".

Although not strictly robots, the Daleks use Robomen to enforce their regime in *The Dalek Invasion of Earth*. The more intelligent of their human prisoners are subjected to the 'transfer' operation, which blanks their minds and subjugates their wills to the Daleks. The Daleks fit the Robomen with electronic headsets for monitoring and direction via radio. The Robomen can function independently to accomplish

SUPERWEAPONS

One of the most notable Dalek weapons is the fearsome Time Destructor, seen in *The Daleks' Master Plan*. The device rolls the nearby time field forwards at accelerated speed, rapidly ageing to death all life in its vicinity, or conversely rolls it backwards, reversing the ageing process of organic matter until it no longer exists at all. It's powered by a core of taranium, the rarest mineral in the universe. Once activated, the Time Destructor will not stop until the taranium burns itself out. This occurs when the Doctor steals the weapon and activates it, killing the Daleks – but also his friend Sara Kingdom.

By far the Daleks' most devastating weapon is the Reality Bomb, deployed from their Crucible space station in *The Stolen Earth/ Journey's End* (2008). The Crucible has a heart of Z-Neutrino energy, which can be flattened by the alignment of the 27 planets that the Daleks have shifted across space using a magnetron. Davros explains: "Every atom in existence is bound by an electrical field. The Reality bomb cancels it out. Structure falls apart."

In a test, the human victims of the Reality Bomb simply dissolve to nothing, and Davros claims every form of matter will be similarly affected when they proceed to "full transmission". The Daleks are to seek shelter around the Crucible, leaving them the sole surviving life in the universe after the "reality detonation".

---

routine tasks, or take direct orders from the Daleks via 'oral control'. The conditioning process isn't permanent and when it fails the Robomen break down, go insane and kill themselves. Future Daleks have subtler mind-control technology, with subjects given tiny cranial implants, which can also be used to kill them remotely (*Remembrance of the Daleks*).

Given their nature as a species obsessed with conquest, it should be no surprise that Dalek science has concentrated on developing a formidable arsenal of high-tech weaponry. Each Dalek has a gun integrated into its casing. In *Remembrance of the Daleks*, the Doctor calls it a "projected energy weapon", explaining that it causes "massive internal displacement" to its victims. However, the weapon has other modes, notably causing temporary paralysis to the victim's legs in *The Mutants* and *Planet of the Daleks*. In *Death to the Daleks*, when their weapons are rendered impotent by an energy drain, the Daleks temporarily replace them with bullet-firing guns.

Remembrance of the Daleks also shows us Dalek tactical artillery in the form of the Special Weapons Dalek. We don't learn anything about its origins or technology, but its enormous energy blaster, housed in a tank-like turret, is powerful enough to completely vaporise two enemy Daleks in a huge explosion. In the same story the Doctor alludes to even more devastating weaponry, reporting that the Daleks' orbiting spacecraft "has weapons capable of cracking open this planet like an egg".

In *The Dalek Invasion of Earth*, we learn that, prior to their invasion, the Daleks had softened up the Earth with a bombardment of germ bombs disguised as meteoroids. Few humans survived the resulting plague, with the peoples of Asia, Africa and South America being entirely wiped out. The Daleks revisit germ warfare in *Planet of the Daleks*, concocting bacteria that will totally contaminate the planet Spiridon, killing all life. In *Death to the Daleks* they intend to fire plague missiles onto Exxilon to render the planet uninhabitable.

The Daleks have also dabbled in chemical weapons. In *Resurrection of the Daleks*, they deploy a particularly nasty gas as part of their assault on a human space station imprisoning Davros. The gas rapidly causes its victims' exposed flesh to blister and deform, followed by death.

"They're brilliant technicians; it was their inventive genius that made them one of the greatest powers in the universe," says the Doctor in *Death to the Daleks*. He's right; whether in weaponry, robotics or genetics, Dalek technology has proved ingenious and deadly. If it weren't for the Doctor's regular interventions, the Daleks' advanced science would surely have enabled them to become the rulers of the universe. 🕸

Above from left: Images from *The Daleks' Master Plan* (1965-66) – The Dalek Supreme; Sara Kingdom (Jean Marsh) begins to rapidly age; the Doctor (William Hartnell) examines the Taranium Core.

Above right: The Reality Bomb and one of its victims in *Journey's End* (2008).

Below left: The Dalek shuttlecraft in *Remembrance of the Daleks*.

Below centre: A tank of deadly bacteria in *Planet of the Daleks* (1973).

Left: The Special Weapons Dalek from *Remembrance of the Daleks*.

Genetic Manipulation

Some of *Doctor Who's* most dangerous villains have dared to play God – with horrifying consequences. But have all their motives been sinister?

FEATURE BY **JOHN DORNEY**

The Borad. The Rani. Davros. What do they all have in common?

They all tend to speak in overly florid language, but that isn't what we had in mind. They're all villainous, obviously. All have a bit of a screw loose, unquestionably. But no, the connection is that they're all scientists – and with quite a specific shared interest.

It's noticeable when looking over the history of *Doctor Who* how many of its villains are experts in genetic manipulation. Taking the traits of an organism and changing them, altering a life form's DNA, this is very much the Whoniverse mad scientist's speciality of choice. The list above is merely the tip of the iceberg. We could continue by mentioning Dastari's work in *The Two Doctors* (1985), or by noting how there's something more than a little fishy about Damon the Atlantean's surgical procedures in *The Underwater Menace* (1967). Even if their focus is largely directed elsewhere, the Doctor's enemies often dabble with DNA as a sideline – Magnus Greel in *The Talons of Weng-Chiang* (1977) may have invented temporal travel and

butchered in Brisbane, but even he found the time to make rats grow unfeasibly large.

Which obviously begs the question: why does this subject fascinate them – and us – so much? Why is it that the other branches of science and experimentation you'll find within these pages can be the province of the good guys, but experimentation with our genetic make-up is confined almost entirely to the powers of darkness? And why is it that this makes for such good stories?

EVEN IF THEIR FOCUS IS DIRECTED ELSEWHERE, THE DOCTOR'S ENEMIES DABBLE WITH DNA AS A SIDELINE.

It's worth noting that this isn't just confined to *Doctor Who*. Many of the founding texts of science fiction and horror are warnings about the deadly consequences of abusing this sort of science. The only thing keeping Dr Jekyll from being unequivocally described as a genetic manipulator is his sheer bad

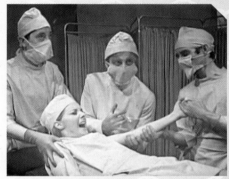

manners in being created years before the term was even coined. (It's something of an irony, then, that his closest *Doctor Who* avatar – Dr Sorenson from the 1975 story *Planet of Evil* – is one of the series' rare troubled scientists who *doesn't* dip his toes in these particular waters.) And it doesn't stop there. In modern days, superheroes like Captain America and Luke Cage are the result of genetic dabbling – and their abilities are sometimes considered more a curse than a blessing – and over in *Star Trek*, James T Kirk's greatest nemesis – Khan Noonien Singh – derives his strength from genetic alteration (as well as partaking in the colourfully named 'Eugenics Wars'). ▶

Opposite page: Nicola Bryant as the part-avian Peri in a publicity shot from *Vengeance on Varos* (1985).

Above: Damon (Colin Jeavons, centre) prepares to operate on Polly (Anneke Wills) in *The Underwater Menace* (1967).

Far left: Dastari (Laurence Payne) and the enhanced Androgum, Chessene (Jacqueline Pearce), in *The Two Doctors* (1985).

Left: Davros (Michael Wisher) commands the results of his genetic experiments in *Genesis of the Daleks* (1975).

Genetic Manipulation

◀ So what's the answer? It's probably, at least in part, due to the fact that gene modification is something of an ethical hot potato. It is, quite literally, interfering with nature (rather than merely defying it, as is the case with things like space or time travel, teleportation, etc, which are largely about finding ways around scientific rules instead of full-on breaking them). This is something that always troubles society. The introduction of GM foods caused huge controversy around the turn of the century, and debate still rages about the morals surrounding the possibility of therapeutic cloning. This gives us our other clue – as we're mercifully free of mad evil scientists in the real world, it becomes clear that in reality both these areas (and others of a similar ilk) are explored as attempts to make our world a better place. They're instigated for noble reasons.

Former script editor Douglas Adams once said that the key to a good *Doctor Who* villain was to make them someone with a sympathetic aim but who goes about that aim in an unsympathetic way. In his own work, for example, you've got Xanxia in *The Pirate Planet* (1978), not wanting to die, or Scaroth in *City of Death* (1979), wanting to stop the extinction of his race. And the epitome of this is the genetic scientist. Most of our villains here are broadly speaking trying to make the world – and their own species – better in some way.

In a number of cases this is obvious. In *The Lazarus Experiment* (2007), Richard Lazarus' titular research involves the extension of the human lifespan, while the misguided interventions of the minute, DNA-repairing nanogenes in World War II (in *The Empty Child/ The Doctor Dances*, 2005) are ultimately medical in intent. Some are borderline. Crozier in *The Trial of a Time Lord* (1986) might be attempting to make immortality possible, but it's not entirely clear why turning King Yrcanos' equerry, Dorf, into the vulpine Lukoser is going to be any use to him. But it can apply to others – the 'curse' in *The Curse of Fenric* (1989) is actually an ambitiously manipulated bloodline that has lasted centuries as part of a plot to free the trapped and evil entity of the title.

E ven Davros' creation of the Mark 3 Travel machine in *Genesis of the Daleks* (1975) is initially about helping his species survive an impending catastrophe. It's just hard to notice this as he pushes it to an extreme, not stopping at simple survival but advancing towards domination and aiming to turn his people into weapons – an abhorrent act echoed in the work of Kahler-Jex in *A Town Called Mercy* (2012), who also experiments with making his people into war machines (with, fortunately, fewer lasting consequences to the galaxy), and in

GENE GENII

ouglas Adams' formulation – sympathetic aims but unsympathetic applications – doesn't cover all of *Doctor Who*'s gene-juggling researchers. Sometimes our villain just does it for fun, apparently, or to show off. An obvious example is Dastari in *The Two Doctors* – the "pioneer of genetic engineering", according to the Sixth Doctor. Dastari's attempts to isolate the Gallifreyan symbiotic nuclei that allow the Doctor's people to time travel are largely about making a god of his augmented Androgum creation, Chessene. This is very much a genius making things happen just to prove he can.

The Rani, the most scientifically inclined of the renegade Time Lords, is something of a (if you'll pardon the expression) master in this regard. The mines that she creates in *The Mark of the Rani* (1985) change her victims' genetic make-up so completely that they become a totally different answer in a game of Animal, Vegetable or Mineral. Wouldn't it be much simpler to just blow them up with a regular mine? Similarly, in the *Children in Need* charity special *Dimensions in Time* (1993) she has a computer containing the genetic code of every creature – which will somehow help her create a massive time tunnel in Greenwich through a method that remains entirely unclear.

MOST VILLAINS ARE TRYING TO MAKE THE WORLD – AND THEIR OWN SPECIES – BETTER.

the Silurians' upgrading of the Myrka in *Warriors of the Deep* (1984). Dalek Sec's experiments in New York during *Daleks in Manhattan/Evolution of the Daleks* (2007) echo his ultimate creator's original design – Sec merges with human DNA as an attempt to avoid the death of his species.

Arguably taking the prize for grotesquerie is Quillam in *Vengeance on Varos* (1985), whose cell-mutation 'experiment' (using the word quite loosely) turns Peri into a half-bird and Areta into a half-lizard. At least this has a nominal point, though an ignoble one – the plan is to exhibit the hybrids as a "warning to women who support their men in acts of violation against the regulations of Varos", a punishment as unpleasant as it is misogynist. Quillam achieves this complex biological alteration through an extremely nuanced scientific procedure best summarised as 'shining a light at them'.

A similar change of species occurs to Ace, the Master and others in *Survival* (1989), although this appears to be more of a natural process. Whether this in some way contributes to the Master's ability to become a silvery snake at the point of death (in the 1996 TV Movie) is anyone's guess, but it's at least in the same ballpark. Other scientists' motivations are plain baffling. What Megelen is up to with the Morlox in *Timelash* (1985) remains a mystery.

While it's true that genetic manipulation is usually

Above left: The Rani (Kate O'Mara) in *The Mark of the Rani* (1985).

Above: Dastari continues his experiments in *The Two Doctors*.

Inset and below left: Areta (Geraldine Alexander) is made part-reptile in *Vengeance on Varos*.

Below: Mr Halpen (Tim McInnerny) pays the price for his cruelty in *Planet of the Ood* (2008).

practised by the villain of the piece, this isn't always the case. Take *Planet of the Ood* (2008), for example. Mr Halpen – the deeply unpleasant head of the organisation exploiting the Ood – receives his just deserts when he is poisoned and turned into one of his own slaves.

By and large, however, the rule holds true. Most of our scientific villains are people with initially positive intent – if not for the world in general, at least for their own species or their specific part of it. These are people attempting to play God, the ultimate act of scientific hubris and pride. It's hard not to feel this is something the Doctor is always going to be distrustful of. It is, in a very real sense, in his genes. 🜨

THE SISTERS OF KARN MANUFACTURE A SERIES OF DRAUGHTS WHICH CAN BOTH ENSURE AND INFLUENCE THE REGENERATION OF THE EIGHTH DOCTOR.

IMMORTALITY

Who wants to love forever? Life-extending experiments have brought terrible consequences to some. Maybe immortality is best left to the experts...

FEATURE BY **MATTHEW KILBURN**

"**W**e can live forever, barring accidents," says the Second Doctor of the Time Lords in Episode Ten of *The War Games* (1969). Thanks to apparently contradictory evidence in later stories, this has become one of the most contested statements in the history of *Doctor Who*. However, the question of immortality extends well beyond the Time Lords and into continued consciousness, extended life and rejuvenation.

Freedom from death has been the privilege of the gods in many cultures. The first person assumed to be immortal in *Doctor Who* is Barbara Wright, who is taken to be the reincarnation of the High Priest Yetaxa by the Aztec priest Autloc. *The Aztecs* (1964) doesn't present immortality as a scientific or technological goal but as a religious phenomenon, the migration of a soul – the incorporeal life essence or personality – from one body to another.

This anticipates a later brush with seekers of immortality experienced by the First Doctor. In *The Savages* (1966), the Doctor meets a self-styled "great artistic and scientific civilisation" whose supposedly civilised people harvest the 'life force' of another – the 'Savages' of the story's title. There's nothing here to suggest that a person couldn't go on receiving transferences of life force forever. This life force includes intellectual capacity as well as bodily vigour, as shown when Jano receives an 'in-transference' from the Doctor. Jano absorbs aspects of the Doctor's personality as much as his energy, and consequently destroys the technology which extends the capacities of one group of people at the expense of others.

The extension of life is bound up explicitly with a power beyond the material world in *The Abominable Snowmen* (1967). Padmasambhava, lama at the Buddhist monastery of Detsen in Tibet, has been kept alive for over 300 years by the enigmatic Great Intelligence, to enable technology that will give the Intelligence physical form. The Intelligence's promises to leave Padmasambhava and let him die have been broken. There's no reason to think that it couldn't have kept his wizened body and tired mind indefinitely.

Mysticism also surrounds the method which extends the lives of the Sisterhood of Karn, first seen in *The Brain of Morbius* (1976). Their ritual chanting focuses enhanced senses, including the ability to visualise events at great distances and effect teleportation. The source of the Sisterhood's longevity is the Elixir of Life. The Fourth Doctor describes the Sacred Flame that produces it as "the product of gases forcing up along a geological fault from deep in the molten heart of the planet". The Sisters are nevertheless prone to illness and injury. Their neighbour, surgeon Mehendri Solon, states that he has treated many of them.

The Sisters' next appearance isn't until *The Night of the Doctor* (2013), in which it transpires that they can manufacture a series of draughts which can both ensure and influence the regeneration of the ▶

Opposite page: The mortally wounded Doctor (Paul McGann) accepts a potion from Ohila (Clare Higgins) which will enable his next regeneration in *The Night of the Doctor* (2013).

Left: Autloc (Keith Pyott) mistakes Barbara (Jacqueline Hill) for the goddess Yetaxa in *The Aztecs* (1964).

Below left: The life of Padmasambhava (Wolfe Morris) is unnaturally extended by the Great Intelligence in *The Abominable Snowmen* (1967).

Below centre: The Doctor (Tom Baker) encounters the Sisterhood of Karn in *The Brain of Morbius* (1976).

Below: The Doctor (William Hartnell) is less than impressed when Jano (Frederick Jaeger) explains how his people, the Elders, achieve their idyllic lifestyle in *The Savages* (1966).

IMMORTALITY

Right: The Master (Anthony Ainley) attempts to restore himself using the blue flame of Sarn in *Planet of Fire* (1984).

Far right: The followers of Mawdryn try to end the horror of immortality in *Mawdryn Undead* (1983).

Below: The dying Face of Boe speaks his last words to the Doctor (David Tennant), Novice Hame (Anna Hope) and Martha Jones (Freema Agyeman) in *Gridlock* (2007).

Bottom left: A publicity shot of John Barrowman as Captain Jack, complete with Vortex manipulator.

Bottom right: An aged Tala (Imogen Bickford-Smith) prepares to regenerate in *Underworld* (1978).

◀ Eighth Doctor. It's not stated whether this presumably technological development has any implications for the Sisters' life spans. As the Time Lords used the Elixir of Life too, perhaps this set a precedent for the experiments of the Master with the restorative properties of numismaton gas on the planet Sarn, when attempting the "supreme renewal" of his body in *Planet of Fire* (1984).

By the time the Doctor foils the Master's experiments on Sarn, he has encountered many other technological attempts to prolong life. The space-hopping, planet-crushing and mineral-extracting habits of Zanak, *The Pirate Planet* (1978), exist to fuel the Time Dams, which keep the ancient, autocratic Queen Xanxia suspended on the point of death while a hologram of her new body develops the capacity to exist independently.

TECHNOLOGICAL ADVANCE CAN ALSO RESULT FROM THE COMMERCIAL EXPLOITATION OF NATURAL RESOURCES.

Xanxia could usefully have sought advice from the Minyans (in 1978's *Underworld*). Their 'regen' machines originate from technology given to them thousands of years ago by the Time Lords. The regenerations endured by the Minyan crew of the ship *R1C*, as they searched over centuries for their sister ship the *P7E*, efficiently restored their bodies from old age to young adulthood, but didn't change their physical forms or personalities in other ways. The lassitude displayed by the crew is a sign of what their captain, Jackson, calls degeneration of the spirit, after regenerating over a thousand times – well beyond the Time Lord limit of 12, as established in *The Deadly Assassin* (1976).

The weariness of the Minyans has a superficial similarity to the plight of Mawdryn and his colleagues in *Mawdryn Undead* (1983). While the Minyans regenerate out of duty, Mawdryn's group have stolen a metamorphic symbiosis regenerator from Gallifrey in the hope of discovering immortality. This has led to eternal life characterised by endless changing and painful physical mutation. The symbiotic dependency of Mawdryn's group on the regenerator is reminiscent of the relationship between the Keeper and the Source, the bio-electronic system which maintains the harmony of the Union of Traken. *The Keeper of Traken* (1981) explains that whoever becomes Keeper lives for a thousand years.

Technological advance can also result from the commercial exploitation of natural resources. In *The Caves of Androzani* (1984), spectrox extends the human life span to at least twice its normal length. Refined from the bat deposits found on the unpopulated world of Androzani Minor, it's a valuable

FACING DEATH

T he fixed point in time is established as one of the fundamental concepts of the *Doctor Who* universe in *Utopia* (2007).

In this story, the Tenth Doctor is reunited with his former travelling companion, Captain Jack Harkness, whom he had abandoned immediately following Jack's resurrection by Rose Tyler in *The Parting of the Ways* (2005). The Doctor eventually explains that Rose had been imbued with the power of the Time Vortex – when she brought Jack back to life, she brought him back forever. Despite living continuously on Earth for over a century since 1869, Jack has not aged. If killed, he will quickly return to life with no ill effects.

Jack has become a fixed point in time and space – "a fact", says the Doctor. It's further explained in *The Fires of Pompeii* (2008) that other fixed points in time

are events which can't be changed. Jack is perhaps an embodied event, the result of the application of Time Lord science by human instinct.

At the end of *Last of the Time Lords* (2007), Jack notes that he bears minor signs of ageing – "the odd little grey hair" – and remarks that in his youth he was known as "the Face of Boe", the name of an ancient non-human entity encountered by the Doctor in *The End of the World* (2005), *New Earth* (2006) and ultimately *Gridlock* (2007). Does the death of the Face of Boe in the year 5,000,000,053 mean that Jack somehow evolves into a creature that could evade that fixed point?

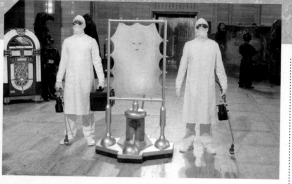

commodity on the populated twin world of Androzani Major. Its price escalated thanks to a war between government forces, armed smugglers, and the androids of Sharaz Jek. Here the search for extended life becomes a squalid battle in which the Fifth Doctor has little influence, focusing instead on obtaining the milk of the queen bat, the only known antidote to spectrox toxaemia, lethal to humans and gradually killing both the Doctor and Peri.

Mechanical methods to extend life can result in creations such as the Cybermen, but also in Lady Cassandra O'Brien Dot Delta Seventeen, first encountered by the Ninth Doctor and Rose in *The End of the World* (2005). Cassandra is at least 2,000 years old and claims to be the "last human", but is little more than a thin membrane of skin stretched on a frame, connected to a brain in a tank at her base. Rose calls her "a bitchy trampoline" who is in denial over the dehumanising nature of her life-support system. By her second appearance in *New Earth* (2006), Cassandra can migrate to other bodies, including those of Rose and the Tenth Doctor, but it's in the body of her servant Chip that she dies.

I n accepting mortality, Cassandra manages better than another machine-aided, body-snatching seeker of prolonged life, the disembodied architect Kroagnon, who takes over the Chief Caretaker of *Paradise Towers* (1987). Better, too, than Richard Lazarus of *The Lazarus Experiment* (2007), who thinks the apparent success of his gene-hacking rejuvenation process means he can sell indefinite life extension to paying customers – before he mutates into a grotesque, energy-sucking monster.

As the Doctor ages, his outlook on his long life seems to come closer to that of Padmasambhava, the *R1C* crew or Mawdryn. The Doctor warns Lazarus that "a longer life isn't always a better one. In the end, you just get tired. Tired… of losing everyone that matters to you, tired of watching everything turn to dust."

In *The Girl Who Died* (2015) Ashildr, a teenage girl in a Viking settlement, is rendered immortal following a rash action by theTwelfth Doctor. Guilt-ridden over his involvement in Ashildr's death in the defeat of the alien Mire, he implants a Mire battlefield medical kit in Ashildr's body. This not only brings her back to life but keeps repairing her. For several centuries, Ashildr is sustained by the belief that the Doctor will come for her and they'll travel together. Her name is forgotten and she thinks of herself simply as 'Me'.

Ashildr lives in linear time until the end of the universe, when she confronts the Doctor about the possibility that he and Clara are the destructive Hybrid feared by the Time Lords. By this time Clara herself is in a quasi-immortal state. While her death is a fixed point in time which can't be changed, she has been extracted from time a moment

before her death and exists between heartbeats. Ashildr and Clara were last seen in *Hell Bent* (2015) in a stolen TARDIS, paradoxically travelling forever if Clara's return to her timeline and her death can be postponed indefinitely – even though it remains inevitable.

Debates surrounding immortality in *Doctor Who* have been as much concerned with the balance between individual consciousness, identity and the prolonged existence of the physical body, as they have the mechanics of preserving life. The Doctor has at times disapproved of immortality, but has played his part in bringing immortals into being.

For the Time Lords, immortality has been a punishment, as suffered by the immobilised victims in Rassilon's Tomb (*The Five Doctors*, 1983), and also a weapon of war – as suggested in *The Sound of Drums* (2007) and *The End of Time* (2009). For the Doctor, however, nearing the end of his life on the planet Trenzalore (in *The Time of the Doctor*, 2013), the granting of a new regeneration cycle is nothing less than a remarkable gift. 🔊

Above left: Cassandra and her attendants in *The End of the World* (2005).

Above right: Borusa (Philip Latham) prepares for immortality in *The Five Doctors* (1983). Moments later he will realise the true meaning of his prize.

Left: The Doctor (Peter Davison) and Peri (Nicola Bryant) begin to suffer the effects of spectrox toxaemia in *The Caves of Androzani* (1984).

Below: Jenna Coleman (as Clara), Peter Capaldi (as the Doctor) and Maisie Williams (as Ashildr) in a publicity shot from *The Girl Who Died* (2015).

A KETTLE AND SOME STRING

The Doctor doesn't always rely on the sonic screwdriver. Often, his solutions to problems are far more ingenious…

FEATURE BY MARK WRIGHT

In the 2007 Comic Relief mini-episode *Time Crash*, there's a moment when the Tenth Doctor passes comment on the Fifth Doctor declining to use the offered sonic screwdriver. "Oh no, of course, you liked to go hands-free, didn't you? Like hey, I'm the Doctor. I can save the universe with a kettle and some string."

Aside from being a funny line, there's a note of commentary here, not only on how the abilities of the sonic screwdriver have increased in modern *Doctor Who*, but also on one of the Doctor's defining characteristics. He has an uncanny ability at lashing up whatever bits and pieces of technology are lying around – or stuffed in his pockets – to provide a quick, day-saving solution, whether it be the means to fight off a monster, locate a crucial element or control an enemy's resources. It's another indication of how the Doctor has traditionally relied on his wits rather than fists – although some of the technological rattlebags he comes up with can inflict quite devastating results.

The earliest example of the Doctor using whatever comes to hand to get out of a scrape occurs in *The Mutants* (aka *The Daleks*, 1963-64), when the First Doctor uses a Thal cloak to break the circuit between a Dalek and the metal floor. A more telling example occurs, surprisingly, in the historical adventure *The Aztecs* (1964), when the Doctor uses the technology of the day to carve a wheel and create a pulley system from scratch in order to gain access to Yetaxa's tomb and the TARDIS.

For the first truly technological lash-up, however, we must look to *The Chase* (1965), wherein the Doctor tinkers with a machine that will allow the time travellers to fight the pursuing Daleks. The Doctor sedately works on his "box of tricks" across several episodes and is rather vague as to exactly what his "thingummybob" will do to their enemies, aside from letting slip that it won't be possible to use it in an enclosed space. This machine gets lugged around the swamps of Mechanus by Ian Chesterton until it's finally unleashed at *The Chase*'s climax, when a Dalek bumping into it causes a small fire that eventually spreads and destroys the Mechonoid city.

Terry Nation, writer of *The Chase*, provides a link with one of the few other fictional characters who was defined by a similar approach to escaping danger. The US TV adventure drama *MacGyver* (1985-92) starred Richard Dean Anderson as Angus MacGyver, a combined physicist and secret agent who avoids guns and solves problems with lash-ups of ordinary objects and the liberal application of a Swiss army knife and duct tape. The pacifist, science-based background of *MacGyver* (which was rebooted in 2016) has obvious parallels with the Doctor, to the point that the series briefly

occupied a Saturday teatime slot on BBC1 in 1989, featuring episodes that Nation worked on as a writer-producer. Nation wrote several of MacGyver's 'opening gambit' sequences, in which our hero is seen solving a particular problem in a manner not dissimilar to the Doctor.

If there's one Doctor who truly delights in the creation of lash-ups, it's the Second. He frequently ends up garlanded with wires and components, consumed with a childlike glee as he rigs up some new toy. This is exemplified in *The Web of Fear* (1968) when he and Anne Travers construct a device to control a Yeti sphere. It's the same glee that we see in *The Three Doctors* (1972-73) when the Doctor enlists Sergeant Benton's help in lashing up a device to keep a blob of antimatter at bay – an attempt that fails quite spectacularly.

Lash-ups can be a useful counter-measure when under siege from monsters in a locked room. There's something inherently satisfying in seeing the Doctor ripping panels off walls and gouging wires out to cross-patch with other ▶

Opposite page: Patrick Troughton as the Doctor, tinkering with technology in a publicity shot from *The Ice Warriors* (1967).

Above inset: The Doctor (David Tennant) offers his past self a sonic screwdriver in *Time Crash* (2007).

Above right: The Doctor (William Hartnell) constructs a machine for defeating the Daleks, while Ian (William Russell) looks on in *The Chase* (1965).

Below left: The Doctor carves a wheel, which intrigues his fiancée Cameca (Margot Van der Burgh) in *The Aztecs* (1964).

Below right: Anne Travers (Tina Packer) helps the Doctor to build a device that will take command of Yeti control spheres in *The Web of Fear* (1968).

IF THERE'S ONE DOCTOR WHO TRULY DELIGHTS IN THE CREATION OF LASH-UPS, IT'S THE SECOND.

Right: Vena (Jeananne Crowley), Herbert (David Chandler) and Katz (Tracy Louise Ward) watch the Doctor (Colin Baker) make a time-loop generator using kontron crystals in *Timelash* (1985).

Far right: Codal (Tim Preece) waits while the Doctor (Jon Pertwee) turns the TARDIS recording log into a 'Dalek scrambler' in *Planet of the Daleks* (1973).

Below left: Craig (James Corden), the Doctor (Matt Smith), Sophie (Daisy Haggard) and the bizarre device the Doctor builds from odds and ends in *The Lodger* (2010).

Below right: The Doctor constructs an equally strange lash-up, to the bemusement of Jo Grant (Katy Manning) in *The Time Monster* (1972).

◄ components. The Second Doctor rigs up a solar energy weapon while an Ice Warrior attempts to blast his way through a door in *The Seeds of Death* (1969), and the 'hands-free' Fifth Doctor uses just a couple of wires in a desperate bid to adapt a freighter's antimatter systems into a means of encasing a Cyberman into a door in *Earthshock* (1982). Some of these technological gambits require elaborate measures to succeed. When trapped in the council chamber on Karfel in *Timelash* (1985), the Sixth Doctor launches himself into the deadly environment of the Timelash itself to retrieve the Kontron crystals he needs to integrate into a mess of wires and components. This allows him create a time-loop generator and the means to repel the attacking guards.

These sequences can be very useful to writers; they can be lengthened to chew up vital plot minutes if a script is under-running, or they can be over and done within a few seconds. Lash-up moments also provide the Doctor with some nice 'business', casting him as the clever scientist, thinking on his feet. It doesn't always work, but they're part of the Doctor's essential heroic character.

O nce you're out of a locked room, you're going to need a means of fighting off the monsters, and for this we return to Terry Nation. In *Planet of the Daleks* (1973) the Third Doctor is imprisoned alongside a Thal called Codal, the pair resorting to a search through their pockets to find a means of escape. The Doctor finds the TARDIS' recording log, with which he intends to "dismantle the circuitry, reverse the polarity and convert to a low-power receiver transmitter with a positive feedback". In short, a Dalek scrambler. This is more than a mere plot device to get the Doctor out of a tricky situation; the TARDIS log was dropped by Jo Grant, who the Doctor believes has been murdered by the Daleks – so there's an emotional resonance that strikes a chord beyond the Doctor just being clever. Jo has provided the means of salvation. The Seventh Doctor even returns to a similar lash-up in *Remembrance of the Daleks* (1988) to knock out another Dalek squad.

Occasionally, the enormity of the lash-up the Doctor must produce is difficult to comprehend. Perhaps the programme's most ambitious piece of technological improvisation comes

CRYSTAL CLEAR

O f the post-2005 Doctors, it's the Eleventh who shares the same glee in a lash-up as the Second. Some of the gadgets he uses – such as a communicator in *A Christmas Carol* (2010) – have clearly been created from a variety of sources and reflect the lashed-up decor of his first TARDIS control room. He looks very much at home in *The Lodger* (2010), sitting on Craig's sofa, festooned with wires as he tries to untangle and refine the flat's electrics, while secretly constructing a scanner in his bedroom. This scanner is one of the series' most elaborate machines created from everyday objects. Somewhere in there is a bike frame, bike wheel, lampshade, angle-poise lamp, digital and wind-up alarm clocks, walking frame, Christmas lights, shopping trolley and brush. In fact, it's entirely possible that it also contains a kettle and some string.

Elsewhere, the Third Doctor was, by necessity, a technological tinkerer, happily sketching a circuit diagram on a motorbike's windshield to show Sergeant Osgood how to improvise a diothermic energy exchanger in *The Dæmons* (1971).

If the Eleventh Doctor's everyday object scanner from *The Lodger* has an ancestor in the original run of *Doctor Who*, it's seen in *The Time Monster* (1972), when the Third Doctor

needs to divert the Master's plan to drain energy from the Crystal of Kronos. The device he assembles to do this comprises a needle, cork, wine bottle, two forks, a napkin ring, various sets of keys, a corkscrew, an ash tray, and tea leaves in a tea cup. It might look like a ridiculous piece of modern art but in fact it's a time-flow analogue to interfere with the Master's activities. As the Doctor explains to a confused Brigadier: "The relationships between the different molecular bonds and the actual shapes form a crystalline structure of ratios."

Well, if you say so, Doctor…

in *Logopolis* (1981), when the Fourth Doctor joins forces with the Master and adapts the Pharos Project radio telescope to prevent the universe from being destroyed by entropy. There's a sinister symmetry to the Master subsequently holding the entire universe to ransom using a lash-up of a personal stereo and an advanced radio telescope.

In *The Parting of the Ways* (2005), the Ninth Doctor has an impossible task – it will take him three days to rig up a delta wave intended to wipe out a Dalek fleet that's only 22 minutes away. The fact he achieves the impossible is another effective marker of how brilliant the Doctor is, but in this case it's a lash-up too far, threatening to fry not just the Daleks but also the humans on the Game Station. When it comes to it, the Doctor can't pull the lever. It's a reminder of the terrible things he did in the Time War, and ultimately shows that, however clever our hero is, whatever ingenious solutions he comes up with, he's a figure of compassion.

There are also occasions when – to defeat a threat at the eleventh hour, when reason and negotiation have failed – the Doctor must resort to an ingenious technological solution. In *Fury from the Deep* (1968), the Second Doctor modifies electrical circuits and amplify Victoria's screams to destroy the seaweed creature, a situation not dissimilar to the climax of *Delta and the*

THE SEVENTH DOCTOR AND A MUSICIAN CALLED BILLY LASH-UP A SPEAKER SYSTEM TO BOOST THE SONG OF THE CHIMERON PRINCESS.

Bannermen (1987). When under fire from the Bannermen, the Seventh Doctor and a musician called Billy lash-up a speaker system to boost the song of the Chimeron princess.

The need to lash something up as the minutes of a story tick down adds tension and excitement to an adventure's climax. It's undeniably exciting in the closing moments of *The Idiot's Lantern* (2006) when the Tenth Doctor lashes together a device to defeat the Wire, using nothing more than what he finds in a 1950s electrical supply shop and an old video recorder from the TARDIS. These are deus ex machinas produced from odds and ends – plus the quick thinking of a Time Lord, of course. It's not quite saving the universe with a kettle and some string, but it's not far off. ⚛

Above left: The Doctor (Christopher Eccleston) is surrounded by Daleks after he rigs up a delta-wave generator in record time in *The Parting of the Ways* (2005).

Above right: The Doctor (Sylvester McCoy) and Billy (David Kinder) convert a speaker system into a weapon in *Delta and the Bannermen* (1987).

Left: The Doctor climbs to the top of the television transmitter at Alexandra Palace with his latest lash-up – a device to capture the malevolent Wire – in *The Idiot's Lantern* (2006).

MEDICAL SCIENCE

From advanced nanotechnology to the restorative properties of a nice cup of tea, the Doctor has come across some remarkable medical treatments over the centuries...

FEATURE BY **MICHAEL COLDWELL**

"**H**e was the Doctor all the time", a good friend of his once observed. He might not be a fully qualified doctor of medicine, or of any Earth science, but his travels have introduced us to a universe of medical possibilities. From miraculous healing contraptions and sinister nursing robots to rare alien antidotes and the humble cup of tea, the Doctor has learned more about medicinal science than any Earth physician could ever know. It's a knowledge he has put to good use not only to save himself, but his many companions and friends.

Let's begin with some housekeeping. Like any good ship, the Doctor's TARDIS (see pages 92-97) is equipped with a first aid kit. It's first seen at the start of the series' third story, *Inside the Spaceship* (aka *The Edge of Destruction*, 1964), when the Doctor's attempt to fix his ship's faulty navigation circuit triggers an explosion that knocks him for six and leaves a nasty gash on his head.

Susan, somewhat dazed herself, retrieves a hinged wooden box painted in a fluorescent shade of grey. From this, she removes a healing bandage – accelerated wound-repair technology in the form of a bulky strip containing coloured bands of medicine. When Barbara wraps it around the Doctor's head, the various medicines inside the device begin to automatically dispense until the bandage has turned completely white, indicating the wound is completely healed. This may have been the only healing bandage the TARDIS had in stock, as we never see another one. Also seen only once in the series is an amazing medicine called D403, drug capsules used by the Doctor to restore life to the stricken victims of the Elders in *The Savages* (1966).

As well as these wonderfully unlikely components, the first aid kit also contains more mundane medicines to serve the story at hand. For example, *Inside the Spaceship* writer David Whitaker needed a means for the Doctor – while still under the strange influence of the TARDIS – to put all three of his companions to sleep, so he wrote in a supply of conventional sleeping pills (presumably picked up in a pharmacy near Totter's Lane). And when writer Terry Nation needed to preserve the fragile health of the newly regenerated Romana on the irradiated planet that turned out to be Skaro in *Destiny of the Daleks* (1979), a supply of radiation pills was on hand for the Doctor to give to her.

With the deus ex machina of the healing bandage and life-restoring D403 capsules conveniently misplaced somewhere in the TARDIS, the narrative likelihood of medical emergencies threatening the lives of the Doctor and his companions suddenly increased. No story harnesses the dramatic potential of this more than Robert Holmes' *The Caves of Androzani* (1984), which depicts the harrowing, degenerative effects of spectrox toxaemia on the Fifth Doctor and his new companion, Peri Brown. Although prized on Androzani Minor for its ability to extend life, exposure to spectrox in its raw form condemns the unlucky victim to a slow and painful death. Unless, that is, they can get hold of the only known antidote: the milk of the planet's queen bat.

The ailing Doctor succeeds in locating a bat's nest and takes a small vial of the precious milk, only to spill half of it at the door of the TARDIS, salvaging barely enough to save Peri. As he accepts his fate and begins to regenerate, he sees visions of his more recent companions and his chuckling nemesis, ▶

LIKE ANY GOOD SHIP, THE DOCTOR'S TARDIS IS EQUIPPED WITH A FIRST AID KIT.

Opposite page: The Doctor (Peter Davison) carries the dying Peri (Nicola Bryant) to the TARDIS, in order to administer the antidote to spectrox toxaemia in *The Caves of Androzani* (1984).

Above: Barbara (Jacqueline Hill) applies a healing bandage to the Doctor's head in *Inside the Spaceship* (aka *The Edge of Destruction*, 1964).

Below left: The Doctor (Tom Baker) gives Romana (Lalla Ward) anti-radiation pills in *Destiny of the Daleks* (1979).

Bottom left: The TARDIS first aid kit is revealed behind a roundel in *Castrovalva* (1982).

Below: The prop medical kit designed by Tony Oxley for the 1975 serial *The Ark in Space*. Photo © Helen Solomon.

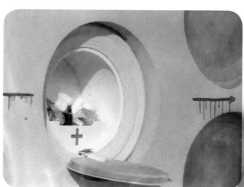

MEDICAL SCIENCE

Above left: Nyssa (Sarah Sutton) helps the Doctor (Peter Davison) with the Zero Cabinet in *Castrovalva*.

Above right: The Doctor (David Tennant) is about to be revived by a flask of tea in *The Christmas Invasion* (2005).

Below: Tegan (Janet Fielding), Nyssa (Sarah Sutton) and the Doctor inside the TARDIS Zero Room in *Castrovalva*.

◄ the Master, although it's reasonable to assume he may also be wondering where exactly he mislaid those life-returning D403 capsules...

Once regenerated, Time Lords generally need to put their feet up for a while and let the new body bed-in, although circumstances have rarely allowed the Doctor that luxury. For Peter Davison's first on-screen adventure, *Castrovalva* (1982), writer Christopher H Bidmead introduced a TARDIS healthcare facility designed for just this purpose: the Zero Room. This zen-like white chamber allows the patient to float unaided in splendid isolation from all outside stimuli.

The Zero Room is a super-evolved descendant of real-world sensory deprivation tanks, which were then in vogue having featured heavily in Ken Russell's science-fiction horror movie *Altered States* (1980). The Zero Room can also be adapted into a smaller, portable unit, as Nyssa demonstrates in *Castrovalva* when a large part of it needs to be ejected into the Vortex so the TARDIS can escape the pull of the Event One. With the remaining section of Zero Room wall, she fashions a floating Zero Cabinet so the Doctor can continue his recuperation while on the move.

If all else fails to bring the Doctor back to full heath after a regeneration, how about a nice cup of tea? Although often associated by the media with the Doctor's 'English eccentric' character, the humble cup of tea was never really a big deal in *Doctor Who*, until Russell T Davies finally called it into action in *The Christmas Invasion* (2005). Having spent most of the episode flat on his back in his pyjamas, the Tenth Doctor catches a whiff of vapour from a spilled flask of tea, which proves just the ticket to restore him to full health. Emerging triumphant from the TARDIS, he explains: "That's all I needed! Good cup of tea! Super-heated infusion of free-radicals and tannin, just the thing for healing the synapses."

THE ZERO ROOM IS A SUPER-EVOLVED DESCENDANT OF REAL-WORLD SENSORY DEPRIVATION TANKS.

MEDICAL MALPRACTICE

In the mid-1960s, some years before the Third Doctor assumed the role of 'scientific advisor' to the UNIT organisation, the *Doctor Who* production team had appointed one of its own. A senior medical scientist with a passion for science fiction, Dr Kit Pedler (1927-81) was head of the Electron Microscopy Department at the Institute of Ophthalmology, University of London (which researched the human eye) and had previously contributed to BBC Television's *Tomorrow's World*. On *Doctor Who*, he forged a friendship and writing partnership with story editor Gerry Davis, founded on a mutual concern for exploring how science in the wrong hands could pervert the course of humanity.

In co-creating the Cybermen (see pages 18-23) for *The Tenth Planet* (1966), Pedler used his medical grounding to pitch the cybernetically modified Mondasians into the realm of scientific possibility. His theory of their evolution from emotional humans to soulless monsters via a process of progressive body-part replacement was a level of implied horror far higher than most Saturday teatime viewers were used to.

Pedler's association with *Doctor Who* proved to be a turning point in his career. He resigned his medical post and, with Davis, created the hit BBC science-prophecy drama *Doomwatch* (1970-72), allowing Pedler to explore many more of his real-world concerns, from the side effects of medical experiments to a range of technological and ecological threats. He remained a high-profile voice of dissent against the harmful appliance of science until his early death. The Cybermen, their eyes haunted by metallic teardrops, carry that warning into the future.

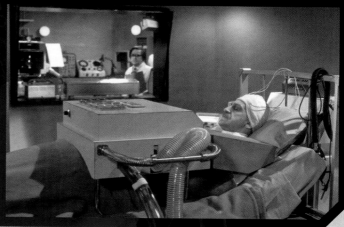

With tea now officially a medical powerhouse in *Doctor Who*, its unique healing properties were further explored in *The Lodger* (2011), which sees the Eleventh Doctor administering a large dose of tea to his new best friend, Craig Owens, to reverse the enzyme decay caused by a rogue time ship that had manifested itself as the upper floor of the house they were sharing in Colchester, Essex. It was absolutely a tea situation.

Statistics suggest that diet pills rarely work in the long term, but, with the weight-loss market worth $66 billion in the US alone in 2017, such facts are, at best, an inconvenience.

Russell T Davies channelled the buzz of controversy around the weight-loss industry in *Partners in Crime* (2008), which reunites the Tenth Doctor and Donna Noble to uncover the truth behind Adipose Industries, dietary miracle-workers whose tagline, 'The Fat Just Walks Away', turns out to be right on the money. The organisation is really a front for the alien Adipose species, who are using Earth and its overweight population to wet nurse their adorable new-borns. Davies derived the name from the type of body tissue used for the storing of fat.

Robot medics are a science-fiction mainstay that are fast becoming science fact. Japan has taken the lead in developing automated nursing solutions with Terapiom, a robot medical droid that can patrol hospital wards delivering medication and accessing patient data. Terapiom could easily pass for an ancestor of the Handbots on the planet Apalapucia, encountered in *The Girl Who Waited* (2011). All-white and humanoid in shape, these benign-looking droids dispense their sinister 'kindness' drugs via hypodermic needles built into their chests.

Also with one foot firmly in the real world are the nanogenes, miniscule robots capable of delivering advanced healing and even complete restoration of life. In *The Empty Child/The Doctor Dances* (2005), the war-mongering Chula species use nanogenes to repair and physically enhance their wounded troops. But as advanced as they are, nanogenes must be carefully programmed to avoid basic robotic errors, as occurs when a Chula 'ambulance' crashes in Second World War London and the nanogenes that escape from it assume that the gas mask on a young boy's face is part of his actual physiognomy.

The concept of medical technology that automatically repairs its subjects was revisited in *The Girl Who Died* (2015) in the fearsome form of the Mire, whose advanced armour has a medical repair chip built into the helmet. This provides an 'immortality charge', effectively ensuring the Mire receive automatic body repairs whenever required – very handy when you want to avoid unnecessary death on the battlefield. The Twelfth Doctor certainly thinks so, and adapts the Mire's technology to human specifications so that the dying Viking girl Ashilda can live on... and on...

When last seen in *Twice Upon a Time* (2017), the Doctor was tumbling thousands of feet to the ground, having fallen from the TARDIS. We know she isn't due another regeneration any time soon, so how she survives such a plunge may well be a new test of her medical know-how.

But one thing is always certain: the physician will heal herself. 🛰

Above left: Scientist, author and scriptwriter Kit Pedler.

Above right: *In the Dark*, a 1971 episode of *Doomwatch*, features Lionel McArthur (Patrick Troughton), a man sustained beyond his natural lifespan by machines.

Left inset: The Mire repair kit from *The Girl Who Died* (2015).

Left below: *Partners in Crime* (2008) features these living fatty deposits from Adipose Industries.

Below: A Handbot offers a 'kindness' in *The Girl Who Waited* (2011).

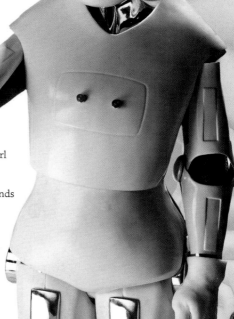

MIND
CONTROL

The Doctor is an accomplished hypnotist, but his enemies'
powers of persuasion are used to more damaging effect...

FEATURE BY JONATHAN MORRIS

"I am the Master, and you will obey me."
Throughout the history of *Doctor Who*,
it's never been enough for the villains to
coerce their victims into obedience. Slaves,
no matter how downtrodden, have an
awkward habit of rising up in rebellion.
How much better, then, to use technology to make people
obey your will; to control not just their bodies but their
minds, rendering them unable even to *think* about resistance.

There are various types of mind control. At its most
straightforward, there is hypnotism; you place your victim
into a trance and give them instructions, before telling them
they will wake up with no memory of the encounter. The
most notable practitioner is the Master, ever since he first
entranced Jo Grant in *Terror of the Autons* (1971). The Doctor
also shares this ability, using hypnotism to save Sarah Jane
Smith in *Terror of the Zygons* (1975) and to scramble Rupert
Pink's memories in *Listen* (2014), among others. And other
characters have also been able to perform hypnotism, either
as an innate ability, such as Captain Wrack in *Enlightenment*
(1983), or as an ability conferred upon them by a third party,
such as Li H'sen Chang being gifted powers by Magnus Greel
in *The Talons of Weng-Chiang* (1977).

Those without the ability can, however, resort to
technological means of hypnosis. At its most basic, there
is the 'hypnosound device' from *Frontier in Space* (1973),
which uses ultrasonics to stimulate the fear centres of the
brain, causing the victim to hallucinate their greatest fear.
Similarly, the Sontaran Styre subjects Sarah to her fears using
a forehead-mounted device in *The Sontaran Experiment* (1975).
More inventively, in *The Mark of the Rani* (1985) the Rani

THE SYCORAX IN *THE CHRISTMAS INVASION* USE 'BLOOD CONTROL' TO HYPNOTISE ONE THIRD OF THE WORLD'S POPULATION.

has a supply of maggots that, when eaten, render the
individual susceptible to suggestion (the implication
is that they are impregnated with some type
of psychotropic chemical). The Sycorax in *The
Christmas Invasion* (2005) use 'blood control' to
hypnotise one third of the world's population
into threatening to jump to their deaths.
And in both *The War Machines* (1966) and
The Green Death (1973) we see super-
intelligent computers hypnotising humans
to do their bidding; in *The War Machines*
WOTAN can even mesmerise its victims over
the telephone.

But the most powerful form of mind
control can be the most insidious. Better
that the people you're controlling don't
realise they're being dominated, whether
it's through the use of an airborne 'anxiety-
inducing agent' as in *The Sun Makers* (1977)
or through the teaching machines in *The
Krotons* (1968-69). Or, indeed, by making them
both obey *and* forget the existence of their
oppressors using post-hypnotic suggestion
(a genetically engineered gift of the Silents,
first seen in 2011's *The Impossible Astronaut*).
Or, rather than overcoming your enemies by
force, why not just make them well-disposed
towards you with a 'pacifier', a device used by
the Minyans in *Underworld* (1978).

If you want to enslave a population,
why not 'brainwash' them into obedience?
That's the approach adopted by the ▶

Opposite page: The Master (Roger
Delgado) is an accomplished hypnotist.

Above: Amy (Karen Gillan) is menaced
by a Silent in *Day of the Moon* (2011).

Top right: The supercomputer BOSS
from *The Green Death* (1973).

Above right: A third of the world's
population comes under the influence
of blood control in *The Christmas
Invasion* (2005).

Right: A Sycorax in *The Christmas
Invasion*.

MIND CONTROL

◀ Morphoton brains in *The Keys of Marinus* (1964), placing 'Somnar discs' on the foreheads of sleeping visitors in order to render them susceptible to hypnotic suggestion. It's also the method employed by the Macra in *The Macra Terror* (1967), where the colony's rest cubicles dose their occupants with a narcotic gas and 'nerve circuits' tap their subconscious minds, while a soothing voice tells them, "Everything in the colony is good and beautiful. You must accept it without question. You must obey orders."

Similar technology is employed by the alien perpetrators of *The War Games* (1969), where processing machines are used to make kidnapped soldiers from history believe they're still fighting wars on Earth. The processing also leaves them vulnerable to further hypnotic suggestion, as the aliens can make them forget or reinforce their delusory state simply by addressing them while wearing a pair of (seemingly normal) spectacles or a monocle.

The Sontaran Linx in *The Time Warrior* (1973-74) uses a similar device to put kidnapped scientists in a state of compliant hypnosis, although, as it's based on a visual stimulus, it proves ineffective on the short-sighted Professor Rubeish. (The Sontarans presumably go on to refine the technique, as their hypnotic control of the workforce of the Atmos factory in 2008's *The Sontaran Stratagem* has no such flaw.) The Master takes a similar approach to Linx to enslave his temporally kidnapped workforce in *Time-Flight* (1982), exploiting the hallucinatory effects of the Xeraphin power source to make them believe they're having a "New York stopover". More benignly, in *The Ambassadors of Death* (1970) the aliens make the abducted astronauts think they're in quarantine back on Earth.

O n a larger scale, in order to gain mastery of the Earth, the Master installed the Archangel Network, a series of satellites transmitting a telepathic signal through mobile phones. This created a 'psychic field' subtle enough to go unnoticed, but which instilled a subconscious instruction to vote for Harold Saxon, not to notice that almost his entire

DALEK DOMINANCE

T he Daleks' earliest attempt at mind control, in *The Dalek Invasion of Earth* (1964), is also the most horrific; termed 'robotisation', it entails converting humans into 'Robomen', radio-controlled via bulky helmets. But the process is imperfect, as the Robomen eventually break down and "smash their heads against walls... throw themselves off buildings or into the river".

By *The Evil of the Daleks* (1967) the process has been refined, with the Daleks controlling Terrall via a small box on the inside of his collar. The control manifests itself as a voice inside Terrall's mind compelling him to "obey". The Imperial Daleks in *Remembrance of the Daleks* (1988) employ a similar device to control the Headmaster, and ultimately to terminate his life.

In that story we also see a girl who has been 'slaved' to a Dalek battle computer so they can exploit her ingenuity and creativity. The Daleks take this callous process a step further with the Controller in *Bad Wolf* (2005); she is installed in the Game Station at the age of five, blinded, her thoughts controlled and monitored by the Daleks. But she has her revenge, secretly bringing the Doctor on board and using interference from solar flares to shield her mind and alert the Doctor to the Daleks' presence. Even at its most terrible extent, the Daleks' control still cannot overcome free will.

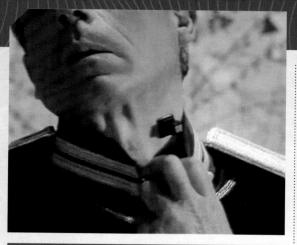

Far left: The Marshal (John Woodvine) reveals his control device in *The Armageddon Factor* (1979).

Left: A Menoptra and Barbara (Jacqueline Hill) examine one of the Animus' gold control devices in *The Web Planet* (1965).

Below left: A statue of a Monk in Paris in *The Lie of the Land* (2017).

Below right: The Monk at the centre of 'fake news central' in *The Lie of the Land*.

THE DALEKS AND THE CYBERMEN HAVE BOTH DEVELOPED EVER-MORE SOPHISTICATED MEANS OF REMOTE MIND CONTROL.

life story was a fabrication, and not to resist once he was in power (*The Sound of Drums*, 2007).

A similar approach is taken by the enigmatic Monks in *The Lie of the Land* (2017), but rather than using satellites, they took one person's consent to domination by the Monks (in this case, Bill Potts), and then transmitted it across the globe via hundreds of statues, filling the minds of everyone on the planet with propaganda about the Monks being benevolent protectors of humanity. But, just as the Master's Archangel Network was vulnerable to being overridden by people simultaneously invoking the Doctor's name, the Monks' network is vulnerable to its 'lynchpin' using it to transmit an irresistible idealised image of her mother, opening a window to a world without the Monks. In both cases, the 'false consciousness' crumble in the face of a genuine, heartfelt declaration of love.

Another drawback with hypnotism is that you have no direct control over your victims; you just tell them what to do and off they go. If you want to give them further instructions, you have to go through the whole process again. Which is why many villains have gone a step further and opted to maintain

a form of 'remote control', controlling their every moment and utterance by radio (or similar). Over the course of the series the Daleks and the Cybermen have both developed ever-more sophisticated means of remote mind control but they are by no means the only ones.

There are two types of remote mind control: where the victim needs to be wearing or implanted with some kind of control device, and where the control can be applied universally. In the first category you have the devices used by the Shadow to control the Marshal and Princess Astra in *The Armageddon Factor* (1979) – small black squares affixed to the left side of the neck. In *Warriors of the Deep* (1984) the sync-operator Maddox has been fitted with brain implants enabling him to link to a computer, a weakness exploited by enemy agents who use a 'conditioning disc' to render him vulnerable to short-range remote control.

There are also the control bracelets used by the Tereleptils in *The Visitation* (1982). These bracelets are designed to restrain captives on prison planets, but the fugitive Tereleptils use them to control local villagers and hear their thoughts. In *Logopolis* (1981) the Master uses a control bracelet to manipulate Nyssa (although the bracelet only seems to control her body, rather than her mind). In *The Keeper of Traken* (1981) the Master uses a metal collar to control Kassia – this device also enables him to see what she sees, hear what she hears, and to shoot energy beams from her eyes. The Animus in *The Web Planet* (1965) gains control of Barbara and the ▶

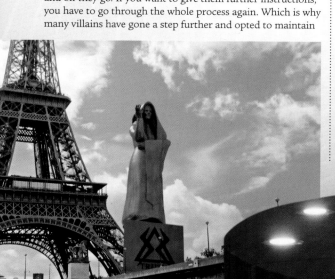

MIND CONTROL

Above left: Edu (Edward Kelsey) and Torvin (John Bryans) are compelled to carry Erato's translator in *The Creature from the Pit* (1979).

Above right: Sensorites in telepathic communication with their home planet in *The Sensorites* (1964).

Below: A publicity shot from *The Hand of Fear* (1976) showing Tom Baker as the Doctor and what remains of Eldrad.

THROUGHOUT *DOCTOR WHO* THERE HAVE BEEN NUMEROUS ALIEN RACES WITH THE ABILITY TO CONTROL PEOPLE THROUGH 'MENTAL FORCE' AND 'PSYCHIC ENERGY'.

◀ Zarbi through gold collars and bracelets. Additionally, there is the crystal ring in *The Hand of Fear* (1976), which contains Eldrad's intelligence and genetic code and which takes over the mind of the wearer, and the Tythonian communicator from *The Creature from the Pit* (1979), a gadget resembling an ornate shield which takes over the bandits Edu and Torvin.

But ideally, you want to be able to control people without the necessity for an implant or bracelet. Throughout *Doctor Who* there have been numerous alien races with the ability to control people through 'mental force' and 'psychic energy' – the Weed Creature in *Fury from the Deep* (1968), Sutekh in *Pyramids of Mars* (1975), the Malus in *The Awakening* (1984). Others have resorted to technology. The Sensorites in *The Sensorites* (1964) aren't naturally telepathic but require small disc-like 'mind transmitters' held to the forehead to read the thoughts of their human visitors. Lilith in *The Shakespeare Code* (2007), on the other hand, uses a 'DNA replicator module' in the form of a witch's poppet to control William Shakespeare. The coronet of Rassilon in *The Five Doctors* (1983) gives the wearer a similar ability, to subdue others through force of willpower alone.

As technology becomes sufficiently advanced to gain sentience, the power to control minds is not far behind. WOTAN and BOSS can only issue hypnotic commands, but the Exxilon city in *Death to the Daleks* (1974) can attack intruders' minds, while the computer Xoanon in *The Face of Evil* (1977) can create 'psi-tri projections', invisible creatures with enough kinetic energy to kill, as well as having the ability to communicate telepathically with its followers and to (briefly) possess Leela.

But even the Exxilon city and Xoanon's powers are only effective over a short range. The most powerful mind control device in *Doctor Who* must be the Conscience Machine of Marinus. We don't see it being operated in *The Keys of Marinus*, but learn that when

CYBER CONTROL

Like the Daleks, you can trace a clear through-line of technological advancement with the Cybermen's mind control. Initially the technology is relatively primitive. In *The Moonbase* (1967) the Cybermen first have to infect their victims with a 'neurotropic virus' before they can be 'converted'; this entails being fitted with 'mind control headpieces' which allow them to be radio-controlled with a portable control box.

In *The Tomb of the Cybermen* (1967) the Cybermen also have radio control over the partially Cyber-converted Toberman, although

this time the Cyberman Controller can issue instructions without the need for a control box. Then, in *The Wheel in Space* (1968), they can use their head-mounted lights to hypnotise their victims, although they still need to issue verbal instructions. Their technology improves further in *The Invasion* (1968), where every device produced by International

Electromatics contains a 'micro-monolothic circuit' which, when activated, creates a 'Cyber-hypnotic force'.

The Cybermen use more radio-control headsets in *Silver Nemesis* (1988), a development mirrored in the alternative universe seen in *Rise of the Cybermen/The Age of Steel* (2006), where they use the ubiquitous 'ear-pods'

to take control. The ear-pods are developed further in *Army of Ghosts* (2006), where they have a filament that extends into the brain. The Cybermen employ similar devices in *The Next Doctor* (2008), while *Nightmare in Silver* (2013) shows us the latest, most grisly development of the technology, as 'Cybermites' are not only able to control their victims but also to partially 'upgrade' them into Cybermen.

it was activated, it could "influence the minds of men throughout the planet", eliminating the need for individuals to decide between right and wrong, bringing seven centuries of prosperity to the planet before a man called Yartek found a way to resist its influence. Following the deactivation of the machine (in order to be modified and thus made irresistible), Yartek attempts to reactivate it to enslave the minds of everyone on Marinus.

Asimilarly ambitious scheme is attempted by Skagra in *Shada* (partially recorded in 1979 and released with animated scenes in 2017). The story concerns Skagra's attempt to track down the Time Lord criminal Salyavin, intent on adding his mind to a mental 'melting pot' contained in a brain-draining sphere (designed to pool intellectual resources through electronic mind transference). Salyavin, it turns out, has the unique ability to transfer the contents of his mind into those of others, enabling him to control them. Skagra intends to occupy the minds of every living being in the universe and become an omnipotent, immortal, godlike entity.

This leads to the final form of mind control: possession, or the transfer of a 'mind' into another brain. The transference achieved by Crozier in *The Trial of a Time Lord* (1986) works by

effectively overwriting the subject's brain (in this case, Peri Brown) with the transferred mind (in this case, Kiv). The 'corpo-electroscopy' in *Paradise Towers* (1987) works on a similar principle, the architect Kroagnon devising a way of non-surgically transplanting the contents of his disembodied brain into the mind of the Chief Caretaker, leaving the Caretaker as an "unalive" body animated by a living brain. The one exception is in *New Earth* (2006), where Cassandra uses an outlawed 'psychograft' machine to transfer her mind into Rose's head, while Rose's mind remains alive but perilously 'compressed'. The process also leaves Cassandra able to transfer her mind to other hosts and access their thoughts.

It's curious, though, that Cassandra's mind-transference gives her an insight into the plight of the plague-ridden 'lab rats', which highlights a seemingly inherent flaw in all attempts at mind control; that it can be resisted and defeated by acts of love, faith and empathy, willpower, self-preservation or even just plain stubbornness. As the Doctor observes in *Terror of the Autons*, "the [human] mind struggles constantly to free itself." ⚛

Above left: A Cyberman in *The Wheel in Space* (1968).

Top left: Jackie (Camille Coduri) is controlled by Cybus technology in *Rise of the Cybermen* (2006).

Top right: Cybermites in *Nightmare in Silver* (2013).

Below left: Matrona Kani (Alibe Parsons) and Crozier (Patrick Ryecart) prepare to operate on Peri in *The Trial of a Time Lord* (1986).

Below right: The body of Rose (Billie Piper) is possessed by Cassandra in *New Earth* (2006).

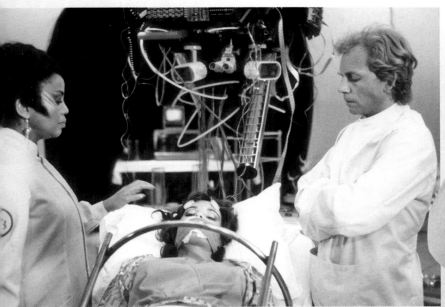

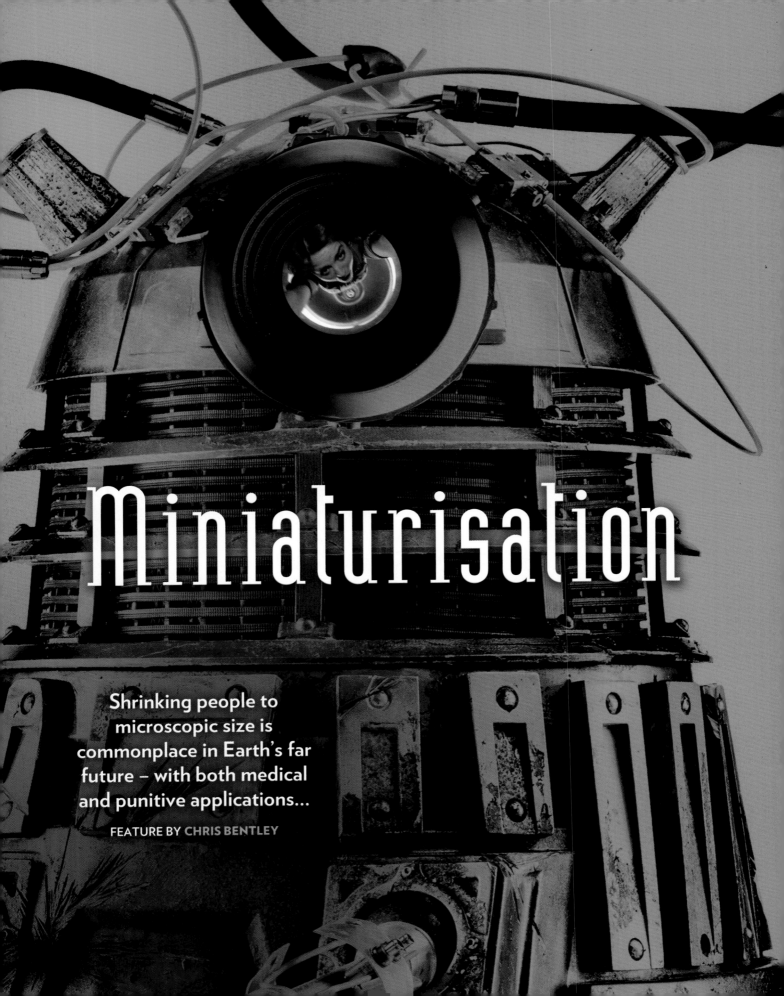

Miniaturisation

Shrinking people to microscopic size is commonplace in Earth's far future – with both medical and punitive applications...

FEATURE BY **CHRIS BENTLEY**

The concept of human miniaturisation, whether by fantastical or science-based means, has fascinated writers for centuries and become one of the most frequent devices in speculative fiction – notably in novels such as Barry N Malzberg's *The Men Inside* (1973), Lindsay Gutteridge's *Cold War in a Country Garden* (1971) and Richard Matheson's *The Shrinking Man* (1956). The last of these was memorably filmed the same year as *The Incredible Shrinking Man*, but, for many, the 1966 feature *Fantastic Voyage* offers the definitive screen representation of scientifically induced miniaturisation.

The film tells of an experimental nuclear-powered submarine, the *Proteus*, and its crew of medical specialists, who are shrunk to microscopic size and injected into the brain of a top scientist in order to dissolve an inoperable blood clot using a laser beam. The principle of the miniaturisation process is unexplained: the *Proteus* is simply bathed in beams of light from overhead Miniaturiser apparatus and the submarine, with its team already on board, rapidly reduces in size.

In his novelisation of the film's screenplay, also titled *Fantastic Voyage* (1966), the acclaimed science-fiction author Isaac Asimov acknowledged the inherent impossibility of such miniaturisation, citing the relationships between mass, strength, organic complexity and the immutability of the Planck constant. Nonetheless, Asimov also provided the concept with a measure of scientific plausibility by introducing notions of harnessing hyperspace to reduce the size of atoms, ideas that he expanded upon in his later novel *Fantastic Voyage II: Destination Brain* (1987).

In the *Doctor Who* universe, miniaturisation is not just plausible but a common medical practice by the 31st century, as seen in *Into the Dalek* (2014). On board the former hospital ship *Aristotle*, a moleculon nano-scaler miniaturises living matter, enabling teams of tiny surgeons to climb inside their patients. "Fantastic idea for a movie," says the Doctor. "Terrible idea for a proctologist."

Sited in the ship's surgical laboratory, the nano-scaler comprises a transparent cylindrical chamber, large enough to comfortably accommodate six people, positioned beneath a moving archway. With the subjects seated inside the nano-scaler tank, the arch passes rapidly back and forth along the length of the chamber, moving faster and faster as the tank diminishes in size. The occupants are advised to continue breathing normally during miniaturisation, as they would explode if they held their breath. Once the process is complete, bracelet nano-controllers take over the molecular compression, maintaining each subject within a personal compression field: a simple button control releases the field, returning the wearer to normal size.

At some unspecified period in the far future – possibly the 52nd century, circa 5150 – miniaturisation technology plays a vital role in the operation of the Justice Department vehicles known as Teselectas. These sophisticated shape-shifting androids can alter their appearance to disguise themselves as any person in the universe. Used to travel through time and locate criminals who have gone unpunished during their lifetime, each Teselecta is crewed by 421 tiny Justice Department operatives maintained in a miniaturised state within a compression field. The Teselecta also emits a miniaturisation ray from its right eye, instantly shrinking a target and drawing the miniaturised person inside the android through the same eye. ▶

> **OCCUPANTS ARE ADVISED TO CONTINUE BREATHING NORMALLY DURING MINIATURISATION, AS THEY WOULD EXPLODE IF THEY HELD THEIR BREATH.**

THE SCREEN'S MOST *fantastic voyage*

Stephen Boyd, Raquel Welch, Edmond O'Brien, Donald Pleasence, Arthur O'Connell, William Redfield and Arthur Kennedy. Produced by Saul David, Directed by Richard Fleischer, Screenplay by Harry Kleiner, Adaptation by David Duncan, Music by Leonard Rosenman, CinemaScope, Color by DeLuxe 20

Opposite page: Rusty the Dalek and Clara (Jenna Coleman) from *Inside the Dalek* (2014).

Above: An American poster for the 1966 film *Fantastic Voyage*.

Below left: The *Inside the Dalek* surgical team wait in the nano-scaler.

Below right: The Teselecta takes the form of Zimmerman (Philip Rham) and miniaturises him in *Let's Kill Hitler* (2011).

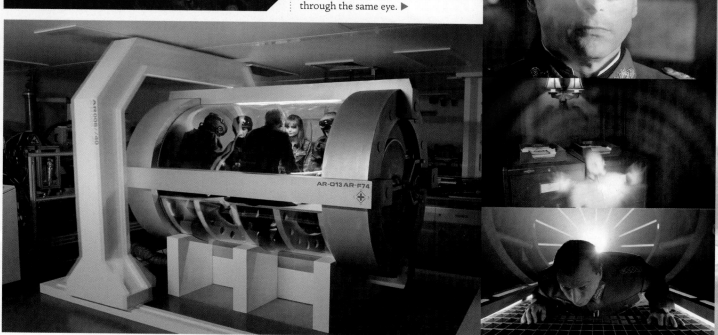

Miniaturisation

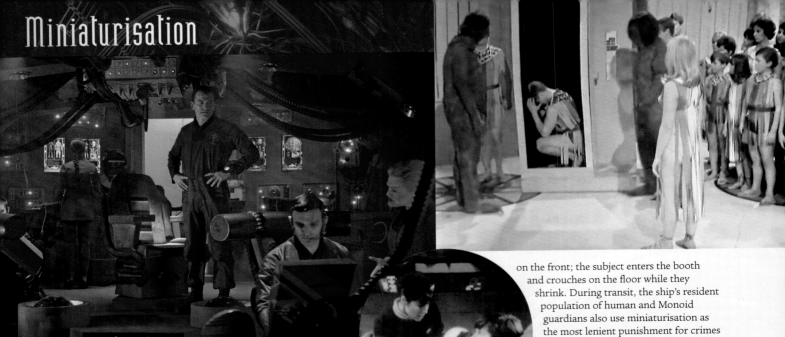

◀ The Doctor becomes involved with Justice Department Vehicle 6018 during a visit to Berlin in 1938, where Amy Pond and Rory Williams are miniaturised and taken on board the Teselecta to meet its commanding officer Captain Carter (*Let's Kill Hitler*, 2011). Later, Carter's Teselecta impersonates the Doctor in order to feign his death on the shore of Lake Silencio in Utah on 22 April 2011 while the miniaturised Doctor hides inside (*The Impossible Astronaut* and *The Wedding of River Song*, 2011).

More than ten million years later, miniaturisation plays a vital role in perpetuating the human race. *The Ark* (1966) begins in the 57th segment of time, when most of Earth's population has been reduced to micro-cell size and stored in trays aboard a starship for transportation to a new home on the planet Refusis II. Reduction is effected by the Minifier, a rectangular booth with a hinged door on one side and a large window on the front; the subject enters the booth and crouches on the floor while they shrink. During transit, the ship's resident population of human and Monoid guardians also use miniaturisation as the most lenient punishment for crimes that endanger the success of the *Ark*'s mission, with those found guilty sentenced to reduction and storage until the ship's arrival at Refusis II.

Miniaturisation technology was also developed by the Chameleons, an alien race who intend to abduct 50,000 young people from Earth in July 1966 (*The Faceless Ones*, 1967). The nature of the aliens' reduction process is unclear, but it begins with their victims being given special food while they travel on Chameleon Tours air flights from Gatwick Airport; the passengers are then shrunk and ferried to a satellite in Earth orbit.

In *Four to Doomsday* (1982), Monarch plans to conquer Earth with a deadly miniaturising poison, secreted from Urbankan glands, which cause organic matter to shrink in on itself. The effect is described by Bigon as such that one trillionth of a gram would reduce someone to the size of a grain of salt. Monarch intends to miniaturise the population of Earth and replace them with his own people, but the Doctor uses the poison on Monarch instead and he rapidly becomes small enough to fit inside the Doctor's space helmet.

ACCIDENTAL SHRINKAGE

Miniaturisation has occasionally been the unintentional result of equipment failure or the mishandling of compression tools.

After a visit to Paris in the late 18th century, the Doctor experiments with directing the TARDIS on a different frequency to side-step the ship back into the middle of the 20th century. When the doors start to open before the ship has properly materialised, the sudden increase in space pressure reduces the TARDIS to minute size, leaving the Doctor and his companions only an inch tall. Following an adventure in the garden of a ruthless businessman, the Doctor restores everyone to normal size by recreating the conditions that caused the miniaturisation in the first place (*Planet of Giants*, 1964).

In the 1984 story *Planet of Fire*, the Master is accidentally shrunk to a fraction of his normal size while attempting to build a deadlier version of his Tissue Compression Eliminator (see *Weapons*, pages 110-13). Operating from a miniature laboratory inside his TARDIS at an abandoned Trion colony on the planet Sarn, he engineers a massive surge of numismaton gas from an active volcano so that he can bathe in its restorative powers, returning him to normal size. Unfortunately, he is then engulfed in flames when the gas surge cuts off.

Carnival of Monsters (1973) features a MiniScope owned by the Lurman showman Vorg. The MiniScope is a peepshow machine containing a collection of miniaturised live specimens – Tellurians, Ogrons, Cybermen and Drashigs – in their own miniaturised environments, all suspended within a compression field and subjected to a time loop. A glo-sphere mounted on top of the Scope provides a live projection of each environment. The machine had been acquired from a Wallarian but its origin is unspecified. It has apparently evaded a recall-and-destruction order issued by the High Council of the Time Lords after MiniScopes were banned and their operation expressly forbidden by galactic law.

Vorg's Scope is destroyed on the planet Inter Minor when the Drashigs escape from their environment and break the machine's stato-fields, causing a catastrophic power failure. Fortunately, the Doctor is able to link the machine's omega circuit to the TARDIS, reprogram the Scope and return the trapped specimens to their original space-time co-ordinates. Once clear of the Scope's molectic-bonded disillium outer hull, the specimens revert to their original size.

O f course, Time Lords are well-versed in size-altering technology. Every TARDIS is equipped with a Relative Dimensional Stabiliser (or RDS), the part of the control system that allows the ship to cross the dimensional barrier. "It's quite simple really," the Doctor tells Professor Marius at the Bi-Al Foundation in *The Invisible Enemy* (1977). "It means I can change shape – large or small as I wish." Structured as a rectangular box with handles, the RDS from the Doctor's TARDIS is fitted to the controls of a Kilbracken holograph-cloning booth. This enables Marius to reduce clones of the Doctor and his companion Leela to micro-dimensions and inject them into the real Doctor's head via his optic nerve. Once inside, the tiny clones explore the Doctor's neural pathways to track down the Nucleus of the Swarm, a power-hungry virus that has infected him.

In *The Armageddon Factor* (1979), Drax, a former Academy colleague of the Doctor's, reassembles the dimensional stabiliser from his own TARDIS to create a stabiliser gun, a hand-operated directional unit powered by a portable battery pack. Drax uses it to shrink himself and the Doctor to a height of about six inches, enabling them to hide inside K9 and use the robot dog as a Trojan Horse to gain access to the Shadow's lair. There, Drax operates the stabiliser gun in reverse, returning them both to normal size at just the right moment to snatch the Key to Time from the Shadow's grasp.

THE MINISCOPE IS A PEEPSHOW MACHINE CONTAINING A COLLECTION OF MINIATURISED LIVE SPECIMINS.

An incidence of miniaturisation depicted in the 2011 story *Night Terrors* appears to have been effected without any technology whatsoever. At a London apartment block in the early 21st century, a terrified Tenza child named George projects a massive psychic field which shrinks the Doctor, Amy and Rory, and then confines them inside a doll's house in George's bedroom wardrobe. There, they are menaced by animated peg dolls until the alien boy's fears are allayed.

Obviously, none of this should be possible, scientifically speaking. But then, as the Doctor tells Rory in *The Pandorica Opens* (2010): "The universe is big – it's vast and complicated and ridiculous, and sometimes, very rarely, impossible things just happen..." 🜨

Top left: Shirna (Cheryl Hall) and Vorg (Leslie Dwyer) with their Miniscope in *Carnival of Monsters* (1973).

Top right: Clones of the Doctor (Tom Baker) and Leela (Louise Jameson) are shrunk by Professor Marius (Frederick Jaeger) in *The Invisible Enemy* (1977).

Above: The miniaturised Doctor and Drax (Barry Jackson) in *The Armageddon Factor* (1979).

Left: Peg dolls menace George (Jamie Oram) in a publicity shot from *Night Terrors* (2011).

ROBOTS, ANDROIDS AND CYBORGS

From Autons and Emojibots to Quarks and Vocs, the robots of *Doctor Who* go by many names and come in many sizes. Almost all of them, however, pose a threat to mankind...

FEATURE BY CHRIS BENTLEY

"I hate funny robots," says the Doctor in *The Waters of Mars* (2009) when confronted with Gadget, the resident servo robot at Bowie Base One. Adapted from worker drones, Gadget was designed for exploratory functions and is operated using auto-glove response controls. The robot has a spherical head attached to a shoulder bar fitted with jointed arms, lending it a humanoid aspect, albeit one mounted on caterpillar tracks rather than legs. It's also programmed with a quirky vocal response – "Gadget-gadget" – which its designer, junior technician Roman Groom, finds amusing.

Later, the Doctor qualifies his antipathy by explaining to Roman that it's not robots per se that he hates, but humans who dress them up and give them funny voices, effectively diminishing them. Responding to the Doctor's criticism, Roman recalls a friend who made her domestic robot look like a dog. "Ah, well," says the Doctor. "Dogs – that's different."

Funny robots were all the rage between 1977 and 1981 when the Doctor was accompanied on screen by his own robot dog, the much-loved K9. In the wake of *Star Wars* (1977), almost every science-fiction television series showcased its own funny robot: Mo in *Space Sentinels* (UK broadcast 1978-79), 7-Zark-7 in *Battle of the Planets* (1979-85), Muffit in *Battlestar Galactica* (1980-81) and Twiki in *Buck Rogers in the 25th Century* (1980-81), among others. Unlike his contemporaries, though, K9 didn't owe his existence to the popularity of *Star Wars* droids R2-D2 and C-3PO, having been conceived – and his introductory adventure both written and recorded – before *Star Wars* had even opened in US cinemas.

As seen in his debut appearance in *The Invisible Enemy* Part Two (1977), K9 was invented by Professor Marius at the Bi-Al Foundation on asteroid K4067. Designed to act as the Professor's own personal data bank, the dog-shaped robot computer has a striped collar, scanning dishes for ears and a tail aerial. He describes himself as an automaton and claims to have no emotion circuits, although he does possess memory, awareness and motivational circuits. His nose conceals an extendable photon beam gun with four levels of intensity and he also has self-regeneration systems which render him temporarily non-functional.

After K9 helps the Doctor to defeat the Nucleus of the Swarm in the year 5000, Marius entrusts the robot dog to the Doctor's care. The original K9 eventually remains on Gallifrey with the Sevateem warrior Leela (*The Invasion of Time*, 1978), but

three further K9s are subsequently built by the Doctor. The most recent, K9 Mark IV, resides in the early 21st century with journalist Sarah Jane Smith and is equipped with new omniflexible hyperlink capabilities (*School Reunion*, 2006).

The Doctor and his companions have occasionally encountered other robots that resemble animals – the Captain's Polyphase Avatron robot parrot in *The Pirate Planet* (1978), a crab-like pool cleaner in *Paradise Towers* (1987), the spider robots in *The End of the World* (2005) and *New Earth* (2006) – but these have been rarities. More common are devices akin to unmanned ground vehicles, such as WOTAN's War Machine mobile computers in *The War Machines* (1966), the Interplanetary Mining Corporation Mark III servo robot in *Colony in Space* (1971), Styre's terullian-drive surveillance machine in *The Sontaran Experiment* (1975), Drathro's L1 service robot in *The Trial of a Time Lord* (1986) and the primary cleaners in *Paradise Towers* with their automotive bicurval scraping blades. ▶

Opposite page: Gadget from *The Waters of Mars* (2009).

Below left: The original version of K9 was introduced in *The Invisible Enemy* (1977).

Below: An IMC robot attacks the Doctor (Jon Pertwee) in *Colony in Space* (1971).

Bottom: One of the cleaning robots that patrol the streets of *Paradise Towers* (1987).

ROBOTS, ANDROIDS AND CYBORGS

Right: Dominator Toba (Kenneth Ives) supervises two Quarks at the drilling site in *The Dominators* (1968).

Far right: A mechanical knight from *Robots of Sherwood* (2014) prepares to attack with its head-mounted weapon.

Below from left: A robotic Yeti from *The Abominable Snowmen* (1967); Marcus Scarman (Bernard Archard) with Osiran servicer robots in *Pyramids of Mars* (1975); the Doctor (Sylvester McCoy) with robot clowns in *The Greatest Show in the Galaxy* (1988-89); a Slab restrains the Doctor (David Tennant) in *Smith & Jones* (2007).

◄ Many of these robots are functional tools which can also act as weapons. The small, domed 'Chumbley' machines used by the Rills in *Galaxy 4* (1965) provide a communications interface with other races, converting the Rills' thoughts into speech. They're also able to operate drill rigging and are equipped with a paralysing ray gun. The Mechonoids in *The Chase* (1965) are self-repairing construction robots programmed to clear landing sites and prepare a colony on Mechanus for immigrants from Earth. But they're also programmed to respond to any threat with violence, deploying immobilising arms and flamethrowers to defend themselves and the colony.

In the *Doctor Who* universe, as in both screen and literary science fiction, such non-humanoid robots are far outweighed by machines which mimic human form. Real-life humanoid robots date back to at least the late 15th century, when Leonardo da Vinci designed his mechanical knight, an animatronic automaton clad in medieval armour, similar in many ways to Linx's

robot knight in *The Time Warrior* (1973-74), the Gundan robots built by the Tharils in *Warriors' Gate* (1981) and the Sheriff of Nottingham's robot knights in *Robot of Sherwood* (2014). However, the more typical style of humanoid robot is perhaps exemplified by the geometric designs of the Servo Robot aboard the *Silver Carrier* spaceship in *The Wheel in Space* (1968), the Quarks used by Rago and Toba on Dulkis in *The Dominators* (1968) or Bellboy's giant robot, half-buried in the sands of Segonax in *The Greatest Show in the Galaxy* (1988-89). And whether by accident or design, all have proven a threat to human life.

In *Robot* (1974-75), Professor Kettlewell's experimental prototype robot K1 is designed to replace humans in a variety of difficult and dangerous tasks, having been programmed for all kinds of mining operations and working with radioactive

ROBOTS IN DISGUISE

Some of the deadliest automata in *Doctor Who* have deliberately camouflaged their robotic infrastructure. The Yeti which terrorise the Det-Set Monastery in 1935 (*The Abominable Snowmen*, 1967) and later fight British Army soldiers in Covent Garden (*The Web of Fear*, 1968) are really fur-covered robots activated by a silver control sphere concealed in their chests. Similarly, in *Pyramids of Mars* (1975) the Egyptian mummies at large in the grounds of the Old Priory in 1911 are Osiran servicer robots; wrapped in chemically impregnated

bandages which protect them from damage and corrosion, they draw their energy from a cytronic particle accelerator.

The Girl in the Fireplace (2006) features elaborately masked and bewigged guests at the court of King Louis XV of France in 18th-century Versailles, but these are actually 51st-century clockwork repair robots with corrupted programming. A brass band of masked Santas performing on London streets in the early 21st century turn out to be Roboforms, robot scavengers and mercenaries who accompany alien invaders such as the Sycorax and the Racnoss (*The Christmas Invasion*, 2005, and *The Runaway Bride*, 2006). In the same vein, the

troupe of clowns at the Psychic Circus on Segonax are robots, created by a mechanic called Bellboy but subverted by the Gods of Ragnarok (*The Greatest Show in the Galaxy*, 1988).

The most mundane – and therefore successful – disguise was that adopted by the robots that arrive at the Royal Hope Hospital in London during the events of *Smith and Jones* (2007). Dressed as black-clad despatch riders wearing motorcycle helmets, the Slabs are basic slave drones constructed entirely from leather.

materials. It's also programmed with a prime directive to serve humanity and never harm it, but conflict with the prime directive causes imbalance in its neural circuits when it's fitted with an inhibitor and ordered to kill. The robot is constructed from an innovative metal which enables it to grow like a living organism: infused with disintegrator gun energy, it grows to enormous size and has to be destroyed with a metal virus.

The aesthetically designed Voc robots aboard sandminer Storm Mine 4 in *The Robots of Death* (1977) are also programmed with a prime directive, or 'first principle', which prevents them from harming or killing humans. The Vocs are multi-functional speech-responsive robots entrusted with the complete management and operation of the sandminer, but the human crew is unaware that the robots' first principle can be bypassed by a skilled robotocist using a Laserson probe, turning each robot into an effective killing machine.

Introduced in *The King's Demons* (1983), Kamelion is a shape-changing robot used as a weapon by the invaders of Xeriphas and described by the Master as "a decoy, capable of infinite form or personality". A complex mass of artificial neurons, Kamelion's robotic mind is highly susceptible and easily controlled by simple concentration and psychokinetics. Using metamorphic projection, the Master is even able to impress his image and personality on the robot, forcing it to act as his avatar while he's incapacitated on Sarn in *Planet of Fire* (1984).

A self-governing Andromedan L3 robot called Drathro, featured in *The Trial of a Time Lord* (1986), is revered as 'the Immortal' by a primitive human tribe on Ravolox, but it's entirely reliant on a Magnum Mark VI light converter which funnels black-light energy from the planet's surface to the robot's underground biosphere. Programmed to maintain the survival system for a trio of Andromedans, its cognitive planning and reasoning capabilities ultimately lead it to determine that robots are of more value than organics.

O ther strange humanoid robots to have confronted the Doctor on his travels include the clockwork soldiers and White Robots controlled by the Master of the Land of Fiction in *The Mind Robber* (1968), the Raston Warrior Robot at large in the Death Zone on Gallifrey in *The Five Doctors* (1983), the Adherents of the Repeated Meme operated remotely by Lady Cassandra aboard Platform One in *The End of the World* (2005), Game Station hosts Anne Droid, Trine-E, Zu-Zana and Davinadroid in *Bad Wolf* (2005) and Max Capricorn's Heavenly Host service robots on board the starship *Titanic* in *Voyage of the Damned* (2007).

In his more recent incarnations, the Doctor has also come up against the triple-faced Smilers on board *Starship UK* in *The Beast Below* (2010), Solomon's constantly bickering Robot 1 and Robot 2 on the Silurian Ark in *Dinosaurs on a Spaceship* (2012), the Skovox Blitzer war robot at Coal Hill School in *The Caretaker* (2014), the Vardy interface Emojibots at the Erehwon colony on Gliese 581 D in *Smile* (2017) and the Ganymede Systems Series 12 Smartsuits at the Chasm Forge mining station in *Oxygen* (2017). ▶

Above left: The shape-shifting robot Kamelion in *The King's Demons* (1983).

Above right: A Smiler shows its displeasure in *The Beast Below* (2010).

Left: The Doctor (Tom Baker) examines a damaged Voc in *The Robots of Death* (1977).

THE VOCS ARE MULTI-FUNCTIONAL SPEECH-RESPONSIVE ROBOTS ENTRUSTED WITH THE COMPLETE MANAGEMENT OF THE SANDMINER.

ROBOTS, ANDROIDS AND CYBORGS

◄ Perhaps the strangest humanoid robot of all is the Kandy Man, a bizarre psychopathic executioner with a metal frame coated in sweet confectionery (caramel, sherbert, toffee, marzipan and gelling agents), which delights in devising lethal punishments for the opponents of Helen A's dictatorship on Terra Alpha. As seen in *The Happiness Patrol* (1988), the Kandy Man was created by Gilbert M from glucose-based substances, meaning his joints need constant movement to avoid coagulation. He becomes stuck to the floor when the Doctor throws lemonade over his marshmallow feet and eventually melts into a pool of toffee and scrap metal when drenched in his own scalding 'fondant surprise'.

The origin of the word 'robot' in Karel Čapek's play *RUR: Rossum's Universal Robots* (1921), and its derivation from the Czech 'robota' (meaning 'statute labour'), is frequently acknowledged in discussions of robotics. However, what's often overlooked is that Čapek's robots aren't mechanical creatures but artificial human beings made from synthetic organic matter – the type of beings that subsequently came to be referred to as androids.

Ironically, the original use of 'android' (meaning 'manlike') in the science fiction of the 1940s described mechanical automata. In contemporary usage, the term is often simply applied to humanoid robots, although the formal definition specifies 'an artificial human of organic substance' (*The Encyclopedia of Science Fiction*, 1993). Usually furnished with synthetic skin, androids are often indistinguishable from real humans, as with the replicas of Prince Reynart and Princess Strella in *The Androids of Tara* (1978) and the duplicates created by the Kraals in *The Android Invasion* (1976).

THE ORIGIN OF THE WORD 'ROBOT' IN KAREL ČAPEK'S PLAY *RUR: ROSSUM'S UNIVERSAL ROBOTS* IS FREQUENTLY ACKNOWLEDGED IN DISCUSSIONS OF ROBOTICS.

As seen in *Spearhead from Space* (1970), *Terror of the Autons* (1971) and *Rose* (2005), Autons are androids moulded from plastic so they can be animated and controlled by the Nestene Consciousness, which has an affinity for synthetic organic polymers. Each Auton contains a fragment of the Consciousness, effectively making them living machines with varying degrees of autonomy. The Auton soldiers deployed during Earth invasion attempts in the 20th and 21st centuries are designed to resemble shop-window mannequins, complete with lethal energy weapons concealed in their right hands. But other Autons are created as duplicates of real people and endowed with copies of the original person's brain patterns and memories.

In *The Pandorica Opens/The Big Bang* (2010), the Consciousness creates an entire Roman legion of replica Autons in 102 AD as part of an elaborate plan to trap the Doctor in the Pandorica. These Auton legionaries have been placed in deep cover and believe themselves to be real humans until they're activated by a sonic signal. One Auton legionary is a duplicate of the Doctor's companion Rory Williams; resisting Nestene control, it spends the next 1,908 years protecting the Pandorica.

The Movellans in *Destiny of the Daleks* (1979) are an entire race of androids from star system 4X Alpha 4. Tall, slim and attractive with dark skin and silver dreadlocks, they wear form-fitting white uniforms with removable power-packs

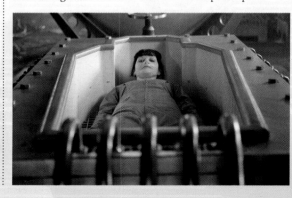

CYBORGS

A part from regular confrontations with the Cybermen, the Doctor's encounters with human/machine hybrids have been relatively rare. Nonetheless, the range of hybridisation he's witnessed on his travels has been extreme, from tech-augmented individuals such as Psi, with his mainframe brain (*Time Heist*, 2014), and Tricky Van Baalan, equipped with bionic eyes and a synthetic voicebox (*Journey to the Centre of the TARDIS*, 2013), to people who have become just a human head attached to a robot body. Among these are the Toclafane in *The Sound of Drums/ Last of the Time Lords* (2007), cruise liner owner Max Capricorn in *Voyage of the Damned* (2007) and King Hydroflax in *The Husbands of River Song* (2015). When the Doctor meets her on Platform One in *The End of the World* (2005), Lady Cassandra O'Brien Dot Delta Seventeen is little more than skin attached to a frame, connected to a brain in a jar.

First seen in *Genesis of the Daleks* (1975), the Daleks' creator Davros is a cyborg whose lower body has been replaced by a mobile life-support machine. He subsequently loses his left hand on Necros (*Revelation of the Daleks*, 1985) and receives a robotic replacement. Prior to the events of *The Pirate Planet* (1978), the Captain of the raiding cruiser *Vantarialis* was extensively equipped with cybernetic implants after his ship crash-landed on Zanak. And in *A Town Called Mercy* (2012) the cyborg gunslinger

Kahler-Tek is a soldier who has been selected for an experimental military program which fuses his body with weaponry.

The Doctor's other humanoid cyborg acquaintances have included Bannakaffalatta, a Zocci from Sto in *Voyage of the Damned* (2007), the Winders on board *Starship UK* in *The Beast Below* (2010) and the Sheriff of Nottingham in *Robot of Sherwood* (2014). First seen in *The Husbands of River Song* (2015), the Doctor's companion Nardole is a former conman and black marketeer whose head is attached to an android body fitted with cheap lungs and glass nipples.

attached to their belts. When the Doctor encounters Commander Sharrel and his crew on Skaro, the androids are engaged in an endless war against the Daleks; both sides are caught in a logical stalemate, with neither able to gain advantage over the other. The Movellans want the Doctor to reprogram their battle computers in order to circumvent the impasse, but the Doctor dismisses them as "just another race of robots, no better than the Daleks".

The Daleks employ their own androids on occasion (see pages 24-29), as do the Cybermen (pages 18-23). Other races that have developed android technology include the Urbankans (*Four to Doomsday*, 1982), the Terileptils (*The Visitation*, 1981) and the Karfelans (*Timelash*, 1985). In *The Caves of Androzani* (1984), the disfigured drug supplier Sharaz Jek is an expert roboticist who creates an army of sophisticated androids on Androzani Major to combat federal troops led by his former business partner.

In *The Rebel Flesh/The Almost People* (2011), 22nd-century Earth technology has perfected artificial humans, the Morpeth-Jetsan company having developed the Flesh – fully programmable matter with a molecular structure that can be manipulated to replicate a living organism in minute detail. Much like the mass-produced 'robot' slaves in Čapek's *RUR*, android doppelgangers of the company's staff are 'grown' in vats and treated like appliances; put to work mining lethal crystal-diluric acid, they're callously discarded like waste when they become damaged. But the Flesh has become sentient, with an energy surge transforming the so-called Gangers into independent beings with the same personalities, memories and emotions as the original miners. The Gangers become indistinguishable from their human counterparts and seek emancipation, prompting uncomfortable questions about the nature of humanity, our understanding of 'life' and the need to take responsibility for the technologies we produce.

As real-world robotics rush headlong towards many of the developments seen in the *Doctor Who* universe, we may be forced to address those same questions ourselves in the very near future – and we may not be prepared for the answers. Perhaps then, those funny robots won't seem quite so hateful after all.

Above left: Psi (Jonathan Bailey) in *Time Heist* (2014).

Above centre: A portrait of Max Capricorn (George Costigan) in *Voyage of the Damned* (2007). The picture is based on his appearance before he had his head transplanted onto a robotic body.

Above right: The Captain (Bruce Purchase) with his robot parrot, the Polyphase Avatron, in *The Pirate Planet* (1978).

Left: Three of the android Movellans – Lan (Tony Osoba), Commander Sharrel (Peter Straker) and Agella (Suzanne Danielle) – in *Destiny of the Daleks* (1979).

SONIC DEVICES

Whatever you do in the *Doctor Who* universe, never doubt that you could be doing it better with sound waves.

FEATURE BY **STEVE LYONS**

Sonic technology is everywhere. There are sonic knives (*City of Death*, 1979), sonic lances (*Attack of the Cybermen*, 1985), sonic probes (inferred from *Doomsday*, 2006), sonic 'door handles' (basically a garage door opener, used by the Doctor in 1970's *Inferno*) and sonic devices to deafen security cameras (*Four to Doomsday*, 1982). In the near future, sound-operated locks will be commonplace (*The Power of the Daleks*, 1966, and *The Space Pirates*, 1969) – while in the distant past, Silurians used sonic lanterns to maintain control of dinosaurs (*Deep Breath*, 2014).

Like many technologies, alas, this one has a dark side. Sonic weapons are standard issue for Martian soldiers – as we learn in *The Ice Warriors* (1967), when one such threatens that his sonic gun will "burst your brain with sound". For larger projects, like destroying a human ioniser base, a sonic cannon will suffice.

The Bannermen employ sonic cones as security devices – destroying anyone who ventures into their invisible fields (*Delta and the Bannermen*, 1987) – while the DJ on Necros blasts Daleks with "a highly directional ultrasonic beam of rock and roll" in *Revelation of the Daleks* (1985).

Torchwood's Toshiko Sato may have been the first human to build a sonic weapon – a sonic modulator – in the *Torchwood* episode *Fragments* (2008). By the 51st century, however, sonic blasters are mass-produced in weapons factories on the planet Villengard. Captain Jack Harkness brought an example to 1941 in *The Doctor Dances* (2005), boasting that it also functions as "a sonic cannon and... a triple-enfolded sonic disrupter." A more precise tool than its name suggests, it has a perfectly square blast pattern.

The most famous sonic device of all, however, is not a weapon at all.

The sonic screwdriver debuted on screen 50 years ago, on 16 March 1968. In the opening episode of *Fury from the Deep*, the Doctor needs to look inside a box bolted to a gas pipeline. The script, by Victor Pemberton, calls for him to produce 'his own version of a screwdriver' – though production assistant Michael Briant takes credit for refining this notion: "We decided he'd get a screwdriver out and undo the lock on an inspection hatch. Then we realised that, in fact, screws are
ut in from the back to stop people taking
the nuts out. So I said, 'I know what he does – he uses a sonic screwdriver!'"

This handy tool turns screws or bolts remotely, even when they're out of reach, sparing wear and tear on the user's wrist. No worries about whether they're flat-heads or Phillips-heads either. "Neat, isn't it?" the Doctor boasts, as he disassembles then reassembles a revolver in *The War Games* (1969). "All done by sound waves."

In *The Doctor Dances*, we learn that he invented the screwdriver himself – when, he claims, he "had a long night" and "a lot of cabinets to put up". He must have been in his second incarnation at the time, as his regenerating first self doesn't recognise the device in *Twice Upon a Time* (2017). These days, the screwdriver is to an extent self-repairing (*A Christmas Carol*, 2010) – but when destroyed, production of a new model is fully automated (*The Eleventh Hour*, 2010).

"It's a little more than a screwdriver!" says the Doctor in 1968's *The Dominators* – a masterpiece of understatement. ▶

Below: An assortment of vintage sonic screwdrivers from the Doctor's desk in *The Pilot* (2017).

Right and inset: The Doctor (Patrick Troughton) demonstrates his new sonic screwdriver to Victoria (Deborah Watling) by removing the screws from an inspection hatch in Episode 1 of *Fury from the Deep* (1968).

Opposite page: The Doctor (Matt Smith) aims his sonic in *Journey to the Centre of the TARDIS* (2013).

THIS HANDY TOOL TURNS SCREWS OR BOLTS REMOTELY, EVEN WHEN THEY'RE OUT OF REACH.

SONIC DEVICES

Above left: The sonic screwdriver is used to create a tunnel in *The Dominators* (1968).

Above inset: The Doctor (Jon Pertwee) uses his sonic to access a lift in *The Green Death* (1973).

Above right: The Doctor (Tom Baker) burns through a lock with his sonic in *Robot* (1974-75).

Below: A publicity shot from *The Sea Devils* (1972), showing the Doctor (Jon Pertwee) using his sonic to examine a landmine.

Opposite page top: The Doctor threatens to blow up Davros (David Gooderson) in *Destiny of the Daleks* (1979).

Opposite page below: The Doctor (Peter Davison) uses his sonic to confuse a manopticon in *Four to Doomsday* (1982).

◀ The screwdriver makes its second appearance in this same story, and, already, it begins to acquire additional functions.

With a few quick twists, it turns into a welding torch. Or perhaps we should call it a "miniature sonic lance", as the Doctor describes it when it burns out the lock of a nuclear bunker – this time with no visible flames – in *Robot* (1974-75). In the meantime, the screwdriver ignites marsh gas, at a distance, to ward off a Drashig in *Carnival of Monsters* (1973).

Colony in Space (1971) marks its first use as a scanner – warning of an "alarm beam" inside the Master's TARDIS – while, in *The Sea Devils* (1972), it "converts into a rather good mine detector". To be pedantic, it's really a mine *detonator* – which admittedly is one way of finding them. Furthermore, with the polarity of its power source reversed, the screwdriver becomes "an extremely powerful electromagnet" in *Frontier in Space* (1973).

By 1974's *The Monster of Peladon*, it functions as an all-purpose repair tool. It fixes wires chewed by a Wirrn in *The Ark in Space* (1975) and operates a (specially adapted) bomb remotely in 1979's *Destiny of the Daleks*.

It really proves its worth, however, in *The Sea Devils*. Four years after its first appearance, the Doctor finally turns his sonic device upon a lock – which obligingly ignites. He repeats the trick a week later in *The Mutants*. "Right," he announces, finding himself shut inside a store room, "if we're to get out of here, I've obviously got to try and break the circuit."

I t's a logical extrapolation of what we've seen before. If the screwdriver can remotely apply torque to screws, then why can't it short out electronic devices by giving their internal wiring a twist? Indeed, in *The Sontaran Experiment* (1975) it appears to use a combination of short-circuiting and heating to destroy a force-field generator – and makes a robot fall apart for an encore.

All this, however, does not a lock pick make. The screwdriver can only destroy electronic locks, as spelled out in *Carnival of Monsters* – and even then, not always. Dalek locks, for example, are too well-built (*Planet of the Daleks*, 1973).

IF THE SCREWDRIVER CAN APPLY TORQUE TO SCREWS, WHY CAN'T IT SHORT OUT ELECTRONIC DEVICES?

Yet in *The Green Death* (also 1973) it opens a "special lift" inside Global Chemicals, without the key that only the director has, and causing no apparent damage. This implies a much improved degree of finesse – as demonstrated again when the screwdriver cracks a combination safe in *The Sun Makers* (1977) without even turning the dial. Before long, it starts to work on mechanical locks too – if not in *The Sun Makers* (it's hard to tell) then almost certainly on the "multi-levered interlocks" securing Ribos' crown jewels in *The Ribos Operation* (1978).

"It's all too convenient… it makes every problem so easy to solve," complained John Nathan-Turner, *Doctor Who*'s producer throughout the 1980s. He ordered the sonic screwdriver's destruction in *The Visitation* (1982), which kept the Doctor 'hands-free' for the remainder of the series' original run. "Before you know it, you're devising reasons why the all-powerful can't be all-powerful!" continued JNT. "The screwdriver can open any lock, except [for when] there's a much more interesting way of solving the Doctor's imprisonment. It had to go."

"You want villains to get in his way," argued former showrunner Russell T Davies, who made the screwdriver a regular fixture of the revived show in 2005. "You want motives to get in his way; you want great big chasms... to get in his way; but you don't want a door to get in his way. It's the most unimportant thing of all." ▶

SONIC EVOLUTION

MARK I

Fury from the Deep (1968)
The original screwdriver – actually the whistle from Deborah Watling's lifejacket, used as a last-minute replacement when the original prop was lost.

MARK Ib

The Dominators (1968) to *The War Games* (1969)
A streamlined design for a device that starts out with only one function.

MARK II

Colony in Space (1971) to *Carnival of Monsters* (1973)
The Third Doctor's screwdriver, reportedly a recycled prop from the 1966 film *Thunderbirds Are Go*.

MARK IIb

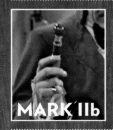

The Three Doctors (1972–73)
A hastily constructed one-off redesign, after the usual prop was misplaced.

MARK IIc

Frontier in Space (1973) to *The Visitation* (1982)
A revamped (or rebuilt?) Mark II, which served three Doctors – with minor modifications along the way – until meeting its demise at Tereptil hands.

MARK III

The TV Movie (1996)
The Eighth Doctor's screwdriver of choice, still with him when he regenerates in *The Night of the Doctor* (2013).

MARK IV

The Day of the Doctor (2013)
Not too dissimilar to the Mark III – wielded by the out-of-time War Doctor.

MARK V

Rose (2005) to *Smith and Jones* (2007)
When first employed it created a visible blue ripple effect, which (presumably for real-world reasons) was quickly phased out.

MARK Vb

Smith and Jones (2007) to *The Eleventh Hour* (2010)
A near-identical replacement for the model burnt out in *Smith and Jones* (2007). It runs off the same software as Marks IV and VI (and others?), as we learn in *The Day of the Doctor*: "Same software, different case."

MARK VI

The Eleventh Hour (2010) to *The Magician's Apprentice* (2015)
Presented to the new (Eleventh) Doctor by the TARDIS; lost by his successor on Skaro.

MARK VII

Hell Bent (2015) onwards

SONIC DEVICES

Above: The Doctor (Christopher Eccleston) examines a patient with his sonic in *The Empty Child* (2005).

Above right: Three Doctors (David Tennant, John Hurt and Matt Smith) combine their sonic screwdrivers to devastating effect against the Daleks in *The Day of the Doctor* (2013).

Right inset: The Doctor gives River Song a sonic of her own in *The Husbands of River Song* (2015).

Below left: In 2012, researchers at Dundee University succeeded in sonically lifting and rotating a rubber disc floating in water.

Below right: The Doctor takes the risky step of using two sonics against each other in *Partners in Crime* (2008).

◀ In the 21st century, the sonic screwdriver is more active than ever, improving greatly upon the abilities of earlier models. Now, it can do more than just detect signals – it can scramble and/or block them (starting with *Rose*, 2005), even reversing teleportation fields (the same year's *Boom Town*). It can remote-control a wider range of devices (including, by *The Parting of the Ways*, the Doctor's TARDIS) and carry out complex rewiring tasks (pre-programmed ones, perhaps?) in a flash – for example, pimping out a mobile phone in 2009's *Planet of the Dead*. It can even recharge batteries (*Father's Day*, 2005) – which makes sense when you realise that its power source must be formidable.

In *The Empty Child* (2005 again), it analyses patients in the Albion Hospital and diagnoses them in extraordinary detail. It's a whole new sonic ability for our list – and yet one with a clear real-world precedent in medical ultrasound.

Starting with *New Earth* (2006), the screwdriver can also interface with computer systems, gaining the Doctor access to the locked sub-frame of an alien hospital terminal and overriding its programming. It can "set up a resonation pattern in... concrete", according to *The Doctor Dances*, and similarly "trigger an isolated shift among the molecules" of a door in the Tower of London, although this means calculating "the exact harmonic resonance of the entire structure down to a subatomic level", which would take centuries (*The Day of the Doctor*, 2013).

THIS DEVICE MANAGES ALL THESE FUNCTIONS WITH ONLY A COUPLE OF BUTTONS.

It can transmit sound through an 'acoustic corridor' (*The Magician's Apprentice*, 2015). It also has a special setting – 2,428D – for regenerating and re-knitting wire, seen one time only in *The Doctor Dances* (again!) – and it heals a minor alien bite to Amy Pond's flesh in *The Vampires of Venice* (2010). Yes, the sonic screwdriver does all this and more – but let's not get started on the crucial role it's played in the various contraptions bodged together by the Doctor. This incredible device manages all these functions with only a couple of buttons and no readout screen, yet remains simple enough for anyone to operate.

This makes more sense after *Let's Kill Hitler* (2011), in which we learn that the device has a 'psychic interface'. All you have to do is 'point and think' – and we might infer that the link works in both directions, with scan results uploaded directly to the user's brain. *Deep Breath* implies that it can also be voice-activated.

So, what can sonic technology *not* do? In *Bad Wolf* (2005), the Doctor is trapped in the future Big Brother house and the writer wishes to keep him there. Hence, the door is fitted with a "deadlock seal" – against which, we're told, his screwdriver is no longer all-powerful.

A further limitation is applied in *Silence in the Library* (2008), when the Doctor confesses that it "doesn't do wood" – adding, in the following episode, *Forest of the Dead*, that some hair dryers interfere with it too. *In the Forest of the Night*

DR WHO'S SONIC SCREWDRIVER 'INVENTED'

So claimed the BBC News website in 2012. Researchers at Dundee University had succeeded in sonically lifting and rotating a rubber disc, floating in water. "It is said to be the first time ultrasound waves have been used to turn objects rather than simply push them." Don't get too excited, though – there's a reason for the inverted commas in that headline.

As yet, the Dundee device lacks the finesse to turn a screw. It's also far too big for the average pocket.

Even so, "This experiment... demonstrates a new level of control over ultrasound beams," said Dr Mike MacDonald of the Institute for Medical Science and Technology, "which can also be applied to non-invasive ultrasound surgery, targeted drug delivery and ultrasonic manipulation of cells... Like Doctor Who's own device, our sonic screwdriver is capable of much more than just spinning things around."

(2014) sheds more light on the former, as the Doctor gets no reading from some trees. "No circuits, no mechanism. Wood... This is a sonic screwdriver. It interacts with any form of communication you care to mention. Sadly, trees have no moving parts and don't communicate."

The screwdriver also has a self-imposed restriction. "Harmless is the word," crows the Doctor in *Doomsday*. "That is why I like it. Doesn't kill, doesn't wound, doesn't maim." And yet – as the Ice Warriors, among others, have amply proven – it *could* do all those things if he wished it to.

The sonic power required to turn screws alone is surely more than enough to burst anyone's brain if emitted at the appropriate frequency. Much of the screwdriver's output, however, is inaudible. It might, in fact, be more accurately termed an *ultrasonic* screwdriver – a name the Doctor tries out in *Carnival of Monsters*, but it doesn't catch on. In *The Green Death* he actually adjusts the screwdriver's output to repel some maggots, causing visible pain to the watching Sergeant Benton, while in *The Day of the Doctor* three Doctors combine their screwdrivers to unleash a Dalek-killing blast of energy.

Back in *Fury from the Deep*, the Doctor cobbles together a device that produces a "sonic laser sound wave", warning his friends that "The sound'll cut you to pieces." He also builds sonic devices to destroy androids when the screwdriver alone won't do the job in *The Visitation* and *The Runaway Bride* (2006).

The sonic screwdriver, then, is really every conceivable sonic device rolled into one – and, being so useful, it has frequently been imitated. Romana built herself a screwdriver in *The Horns of Nimon* (1979-80), while Amy Pond and River Song constructed a 'sonic probe' and a 'sonic trowel' respectively in *The Girl Who Waited* (2011) and *The Husbands of River Song* (2015). The Doctor built a more familiar-looking screwdriver for River, and may also have provided Sarah Jane Smith with her 'sonic lipstick' (*The Sarah Jane Adventures*). The origins of Miss Foster's 'sonic pen' – described by the Doctor as "identical" to his own device – are rather more hazy (*Partners in Crime*, 2008).

Even Missy abandoned the laser screwdriver she wielded as the Master, to sonically upgrade her umbrella (*World Enough and Time*, 2017) – while the Doctor himself utilised a sonic cane for a change in *Let's Kill Hitler*, and sonic sunglasses regularly from *The Magician's Apprentice* onwards. These seem to have all the functions of the sonic screwdriver, with the added advantage of a visual display – and of course they don't spoil the line of your jacket.

With a brand-new Doctor about to settle into the role, it remains to be seen what her sonic device of preference will be. She has plenty of options. ⚛

Above: River Song (Alex Kingston) with the Doctor, holding his sonic cane in *Let's Kill Hitler* (2011).

Below left: Sarah Jane Smith (Elisabeth Sladen) with her sonic lipstick, in a publicity shot from the first series of *The Sarah Jane Adventures* (2007).

Below right and inset: Bill Potts (Pearl Mackie) with the Doctor (Peter Capaldi) in *The Pyramid at the End of the World* (2017). The Doctor uses his sonic sunglasses to hide the fact that his is blind, and to get information about his surroundings.

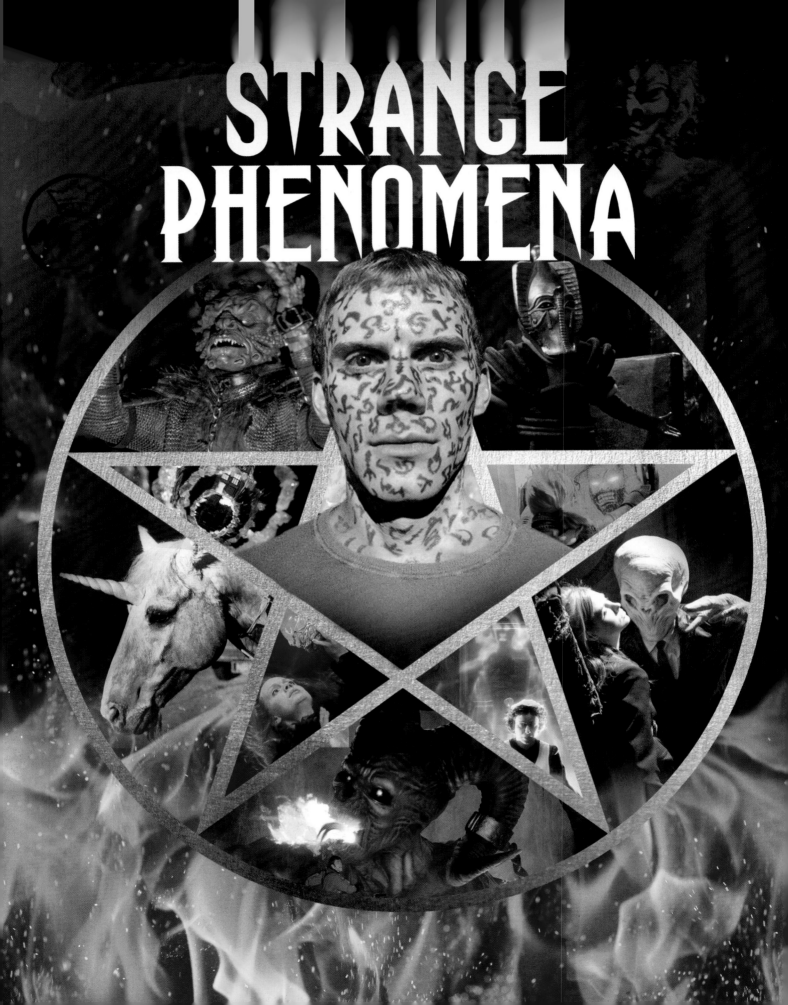

STRANGE PHENOMENA

Science has generally triumphed over magic in the history of *Doctor Who*, but what about characters and situations that defy scientific explanation?

FEATURE BY **ROBERT FAIRCLOUGH**

In his 1962 essay 'Hazards of Prophecy: Failure and Imagination', Arthur C Clarke outlined a theory that was to have a major impact on science-fiction and fantasy writing – that any sufficiently advanced technology is indistinguishable from magic. It was first directly referenced by *Doctor Who* in *The Pirate Planet* (1978), when the Captain discusses the *Ventarialis*: "Now there was a ship. The greatest raiding cruiser ever built. And I built it… with technology so far advanced you would not be able to distinguish it from magic."

This definition explains how the scientists in Salamander's underground base in *The Enemy of the World* (1967-68) are able to (somehow) cause natural disasters, how the Isolus (*Fear Her*, 2006) is able to use ionic power to imprison people in a child's drawings, and how a quantum shade works in *Face the Raven* (2015). In general, though, most of the strange phenomena in *Doctor Who* have a common denominator – the psychic or the paranormal, usually linked to godlike entities or immortal beings.

Fenric, a formless evil since the dawn of time (*The Curse of Fenric*, 1989), possesses the power to manipulate the time lines of generations of humans, as well as transporting the Seventh Doctor's companion Ace and the Ancient Haemovore through time and space. Fenric also has the ability – another common practice of advanced life forms in *Doctor Who* – to possess human hosts. The demonic Beast in *The Impossible Planet/The Satan Pit* (2006) is as impossibly old as Fenric and able to project its mind into the archaeologist Toby Zed and a Sanctuary Base's crew of Ood, turning them all into killers. Similar possessions by higher life forms can be seen throughout the series, notably in *The Unquiet Dead* (2005).

At the top of the cosmic evolutionary scale are the Eternals from 1983's *Enlightenment,* who inhabit what one of them describes as "the endless wastes of eternity". These mental giants are able to read minds, conjure objects from thin air and hide machines as advanced as the TARDIS, as well as assuming human form as a diversion from the boredom of eternal life. *The Celestial Toymaker* (1966) is a similar immortal with a tendency towards ennui. He has the mind power to build his own world and

transform the losers in his games into toys, as well as making people invisible and incorporeal.

These beings share some intriguingly similar characteristics. Both the Eternals and apparently the Toymaker are dependent on the imagination of humans, or "Ephemerals", as creative fuel – the Fifth Doctor says, "Without us, [the Eternals are] empty nothings." In their race for Enlightenment, the creatures plunder the nautical history of Earth in addition to acquiring ion drive and solar wind technology. Similarly, the Toymaker's personal appearance, together with the furnishings in his 'Toyroom' and his all-important games – deadly versions of blind man's buff, ballroom dancing and hopscotch – are all informed by Earth culture.

Another entity dependent on human creativity is the supercomputer that runs the Land of Fiction in 1968's *The Mind Robber.* In a realm outside the time-space dimension, it mines the imagination of a writer for the *Ensign* penny dreadful, using him to turn fictional figures such as Lemuel Gulliver, Rapunzel and unicorns into reality. The Gods of Ragnarok share a similar desire, feeding off the entertainment value of the acts in the Psychic Circus they ▶

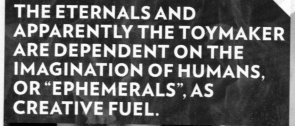
THE ETERNALS AND APPARENTLY THE TOYMAKER ARE DEPENDENT ON THE IMAGINATION OF HUMANS, OR "EPHEMERALS", AS CREATIVE FUEL.

Opposite page, clockwise from centre: The possessed Toby Zed (Will Thorp) in *The Satan Pit* (2006); Sutekh (Gabriel Woolf), last of the Osirans in *Pyramids of Mars* (1975); a drawing of Chloe Webber's father comes to life in *Fear Her* (2007); Amy Pond (Karen Gillan) is menaced by a Silent in *Day of the Moon* (2011); Gwyneth (Eve Myles) makes contact with the Gelth in *The Unquiet Dead* (2005); the Doctor (David Tennant) confronts the Beast in *The Satan Pit*; Lilith (Christina Cole) the Carrionite in *The Shakespeare Code* (2007); the unicorn in *The Mind Robber* (1968); the TARDIS is drawn into the Mandragora Helix in *The Masque of Mandragora* (1976); the Destroyer (Marek Anton) in *Battlefield* (1989).

Above: The amplifier used by Captain Wrack to destroy her opponents in *Enlightenment* (1983).

Below left: Jean (Joann Kenny) and Phyllis (Joanne Bell) become vampiric Haemovores when they succumb to *The Curse of Fenric* (1989).

Below right: Sergeant Rugg (Campbell Singer) and Mrs Wiggs (Carmen Silvera) are given orders by the Toymaker (Michael Gough) in *The Dancing Floor*, the third episode of *The Celestial Toymaker* (1966).

Above left: Mother Bloodtide (Linda Clark) and Mother Doomfinger (Amanda Lawrence), two of the Carrionites in *The Shakespeare Code*.

Above right: The animated gargoyle Bok (Stanley Mason) in *The Dæmons* (1971).

Right inset: Kronos (Marc Boyle) emerges from its crystal in *The Time Monster* (1972).

Below left: The Doctors (Jon Pertwee and Patrick Troughton) explore Omega's world in *The Three Doctors* (1972-73).

Below right: The deranged Omega (Stephen Thorne) in *The Three Doctors*.

Bottom right: Rose (Billie Piper) and the Doctor (David Tennant) stand in awe of a black hole in *The Impossible Planet* (2006).

◀ parasitically control in *The Greatest Show in the Galaxy* (1988).

The alien thirst for human literary inventiveness is also shared by the Carrionites, who exploit the imagination of William Shakespeare in *The Shakespeare Code* (2007). Their intention is to use a phrase inserted in Shakespeare's lost play *Love's Labour's Won* – "betwixt Dravidian shores and linear 5-9-3-0-1-6-7 point 0-2, and strikes the fulsome grove of Rexel 4" – to open a portal to Earth for their Carrionite sisters. The creatures' trappings of witchcraft – mind reading, broomsticks, spells and voodoo-style effigies to attack or control people – represent one of the series' many examples of explaining myths or the supernatural in a science-fiction context.

The first example, 1971's *The Dæmons*, explored the occult in a daring way for Saturday tea-time entertainment. The black magic ritual, the Sabbat, elemental spirits, mysterious, powerful winds and the animation of a stone gargoyle are all rationally explained by the Third Doctor as "remnants of the [Dæmons'] advanced science". The story scored another significant first for *Doctor Who* in showing interference

in human evolution by alien explorers, to the extent that the extra-terrestrials entered mythology as beings to be feared or worshipped, in the Dæmons' case as various cultures' interpretations of the Devil.

The following year's *The Time Monster* addressed the Greek myths, with the explanation that the Titan god Kronos – the father of Zeus, Poseidon, Hades, Hestia, Demeter and Hera – is another immortal being, a Chronovore and 'time eater' existing outside time and space. Significantly, *The Time Monster* is the series' only example of ancient man taming a paranormal force: despite Kronos' immense power, the priests of Atlantis were able, in some mystical fashion, to bring Kronos into time and harness the creature to a crystal in the Temple of Poseidon. Kronos is controlled by 'comparative ratios' on the Seal of the Priest, making this an attractive tool in the Master's quest for universal domination.

The long-lived, psychic Osirans in the 1975 story *Pyramids of Mars* rival the Dæmons for their impact on human culture. According to the Doctor, their imprisoning of Sutekh (another variation on the Devil) in Egypt resulted in "the whole of Egyptian culture [being] founded upon the Osiran pattern", particularly with regard to the building of pyramids.

BREAKING THE LAWS

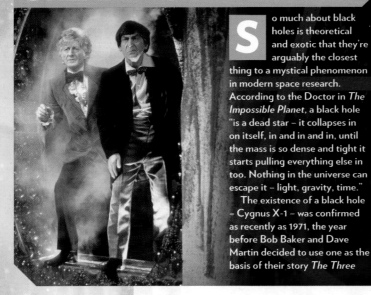

S o much about black holes is theoretical and exotic that they're arguably the closest thing to a mystical phenomenon in modern space research. According to the Doctor in *The Impossible Planet*, a black hole "is a dead star – it collapses in on itself, in and in and in, until the mass is so dense and tight it starts pulling everything else in too. Nothing in the universe can escape it – light, gravity, time."

The existence of a black hole – Cygnus X-1 – was confirmed as recently as 1971, the year before Bob Baker and Dave Martin decided to use one as the basis of their story *The Three*

Doctors (1972-73). The writers drew on established theory, namely that at the centre of a black hole is a gravitational singularity: this one-dimensional point is essentially a huge mass in an infinitely small space, where the laws of physics cease to operate.

Baker and Martin combined the theory with fantasy, defining their singularity as the power source used by the rebel Time Lord Omega to effect an energy drain on the rest of the universe; additionally,

Omega's antimatter world and its physical laws are sustained by his force of will. Appropriately enough, the rigorously scientific Third Doctor describes his experience of Omega's domain in the black hole as visiting "an anomaly within an impossibility".

Curiously for such advanced races, neither the Dæmons nor the Osirans completely abandon conventional technology: the former use spacecraft weighing 750 tons that can be reduced to a fraction of their size, while Sutekh controls servicer robots through a particle accelerator, possesses the components to build and launch a missile and, like the Dæmons, can construct a force barrier, albeit with equipment concealed in canopic burial jars. In *Ghost Light* (1989), the ancient being Light needs a stone spacecraft in order to travel – "at the speed of thought" – even though it's also able to teleport, apparently through mental power.

N o such technological limitations affect two other influences on humankind. In *The Masque of Mandragora* (1976), the Doctor describes the Mandragora Helix as "a spiral of pure energy that radiates outwards in ways no one understands" with "a controlling intelligence" at its centre. This energy is able to impersonate the Roman cult of Demnos in 15th-century Italy and applies 'astral force' to control its disciple. A key part of this strategy is using what the Doctor calls the "sub-thermal recombination of ionised plasma" to rebuild the temple of Demnos – as well as granting the cult the ability to fire bolts of fire from their fingers. In *Image of the Fendahl* (1977), the life-devouring horror from Time Lord mythology is able to project itself across space with energy stored in a pentagram, a five-pointed star that's part of the structure of its skull. Thanks to the Fendahl's arrival on Earth, the creature influenced humankind's dark side, while the pentagram became a symbol of power in occult lore.

The psychic equal of the Time Lords, the Sisterhood of Karn (introduced in *The Brain of Morbius,* 1976) have their own mythological trappings, namely telepathic powers generated by ceremonies based around the worship of the Sacred Flame which produces the Elixir of Life – the consumption of which makes them immortal. The Sisterhood can use their awesome mental powers to wreck spacecraft, kill, read minds and make telekinetic visits. Another religious order, The Silence (first seen in *The Impossible Astronaut,* 2011), also advocates psychic powers, using its genetically engineered Silents to manipulate other species, primarily through the hypnotic ability to make them forget the creatures even existed.

Left: The ancient being known as Light (John Hallam) in *Ghost Light* (1989).

Bottom left: The Fendahl core (Wanda Ventham) looms over the body of Max Stael (Scott Fredericks) in *Image of the Fendahl* (1977).

Below: Morgaine (Jean Marsh), a witch from another dimension, in *Battlefield*.

THE ANCIENT BEING LIGHT NEEDS A STONE SPACECRAFT IN ORDER TO TRAVEL "AT THE SPEED OF THOUGHT".

Doctor Who's most explicit presentation of science-as-magic came in 1989's *Battlefield*, a story inspired by the legends of King Arthur and the Knights of the Round Table. Here, the sorceress Morgaine, her son Mordred and various knights are revealed as coming from a parallel dimension and their science is explicitly defined along magical lines. Morgaine possesses the ability to read minds, cure blindness and imprison the demon-like Destroyer in chains made of silver, a traditional magical protection; fittingly, the Brigadier uses a silver bullet to destroy the creature. Ace is also able to shield herself and Shou Yuing from Morgaine in a chalk circle, a traditional magical 'enchantment'.

More than any other story, *Battlefield* bears out the Doctor's assertion in *The Time Monster* that when primitive cultures are confronted by something they can't understand, "they would invent a legend to tame it". More often than not, legend would claim the unknowable – scientific or otherwise – as magical or mystical. ⚛

SUSPENDED ANIMATION

The technology to freeze all bodily functions and thus survive for centuries is one that many races have employed...

FEATURE BY ALISTAIR McGOWN

Although *Doctor Who* has included many examples of scientific approaches to suspended animation, the programme has also featured several species that can survive freezing naturally.

In *The Seeds of Doom* (1976), for example, Krynoid seed pods thaw out and germinate after 20,000 years in the Antarctic permafrost, while *The Ice Warriors* (1967) have an affinity with colder temperatures that enables them to be frozen and revived. Trapped in an avalanche at least 10,000 years before, Martian leader Varga

is thawed from a block of ice by the Britannicus ice base team and quickly revives his fellow frozen crew members. We only discover much later that Martians possess cryogenic freezing technology on their home planet.

Other races possess apparently innate powers to suspend life. In *The Sensorites* (1964), the telepathic creatures of the Sense-Sphere place a 28th-century Earth spaceship crew in a sleep state. Astronaut Carol Richmond describes it as "a deep sleep which gives the appearance of death". Which life functions are suspended is debatable, with the humans remaining warm to the touch and the Sensorites returning

periodically to feed them. The crew can be revived with a small heart resuscitator placed on their chests. Time Lords can also suspend their own life functions naturally; in *Destiny of the Daleks* (1979), Romana halts all outward life signs, having been taught at school how to stop her hearts.

Doctor Who's first apparent example of technologically assisted suspended animation, seen in *The Keys of Marinus* (1964), remains unexplained. In this story, four apparently human soldiers in medieval garb, standing frozen while guarding a block of ice containing the third key of the Marinus Conscience machine, come to life to pursue intruders when the block is thawed using geothermal hot pipes.

In a more adequately explained process of suspended animation, the Moroks intend

to preserve the Doctor and his companions as motionless specimens in *The Space Museum* (1965). Subjects are restrained in a 'preparation room' behind a glass panel, with the controls encased in a glass dome. The Doctor's temperature is reduced several hundred degrees below freezing, although his mind remains active.

Similarly, in *The Crimson Horror* (2013) the prizewinning Victorian chemist Mrs Gillyflower seeks to preserve and display chosen individuals by holding them motionless under huge bell jars so they can be revived in her distorted idea of Utopia, once she has destroyed the rest of the human race. Her living 'waxworks' are embalmed in chemicals founded on the venom of a prehistoric leech creature, which paralyses movement and function, creating a living death.

W hile the above processes use freezing or chemical means, other preservation techniques are more opaque. In *The Faceless Ones* (1967), the tragic Chameleons assume the identities of young airline passengers. The 'originals' are shrunk by means of miniaturising chambers on the Chameleon Tours aircraft, then stored in cabinet drawers aboard their spaceship. (See *Miniaturisation*, pages 52-55.)

Also stored in a drawer, though at life size, is Victorian policeman Inspector Mackenzie in *Ghost Light* (1989). An alien calling himself Josiah Smith stores Mackenzie – "preserved, hypnotised" as the Doctor puts it – for two years when the policeman investigates Smith's mysterious house, Gabriel Chase. The Doctor wakes Mackenzie within ten minutes, the policeman appearing to have suffered no ill effects other than incredible hunger.

Cryogenic suspended animation is often used for enforced hibernation, with armies or entire races preserved in order to await more favourable conditions, including the Cybermen, Daleks and Ice Warriors. In *The Tomb of the Cybermen* (1967), the Cybermen have slept below the surface of Telos for 500 years, fearing extinction after the destruction of their home planet, Mondas. Their tiered plastic cocoons are likened to bees' honeycombs, with their control panel based on sequential logic designed to trap suitable new additions to the Cyber race. The stored Cybermen are covered in patches of ice, suggesting a cryogenic process. The controls melt this ▶

MRS GILLYFLOWER SEEKS TO PRESERVE AND DISPLAY CHOSEN INDIVIDUALS BY HOLDING THEM MOTIONLESS UNDER HUGE BELL JARS.

Left: Concept art by Shaun Williams, illustrating the cryo chamber from *A Christmas Carol* (2010).

Opposite page inset: Knights in suspended animation from *The Snows of Terror*, the fourth episode of *The Keys of Marinus* (1964).

Top: Clara (Jenna Coleman) and a well-dressed gentleman are preserved inside a bell jar in *The Crimson Horror* (2013).

Right: Two Cybermen menace Flast (Faith Brown) the Cryon in *Attack of the Cybermen* (1985).

Far right: The Ice Warriors' sleep chambers in *Empress of Mars* (2017).

Bottom left: Gerald Harper stars as the title character in *Adam Adamant Lives!* (1966-67).

Bottom centre: The August 1928 edition of *Amazing Stories*, featuring Buck Rogers.

Bottom right: Hypersleep in Ridley Scott's 1979 film *Alien*.

◄ ice within seconds, the revived Cybermen emerging from behind plastic sheet windows.

Attack of the Cybermen (1985) introduces the Cryons, near-extinct natives of Telos. They live in low temperatures and their superior refrigeration technology has allowed them to build freezing cities. These skills bring the Cybermen to Telos, adapting Cryon technology for their 'tombs'; the revivification process proves unstable, however, and sends Cybermen haywire. Whether the Cryons – their name notwithstanding – actually utilise cryogenic processes remains unclear.

In *Planet of the Daleks* (1973), an army of 10,000 Daleks is strategically frozen on the jungle planet Spiridon, utilising a cave system cooled to below zero by refrigeration units, no doubt tapping into the planet's naturally occurring network of ice tunnels. The Doctor and the Thals eventually entomb the army in a torrent of molten ice.

Presumably to avoid imminent disaster, Martian warriors have undergone a similar form of hibernation in *Empress of Mars* (2017), with possibly hundreds of sleep chambers built high into the cave walls of a hive hibernation system underneath the Martian north pole. Their Ice Queen, Iraxxa, is revived from her golden sarcophagus when it's tampered with, the thin outer layer of gold flaking away. Having slept for 5,000 years, longer than intended, the Martians find their planet uninhabitable on waking.

In *Doctor Who and the Silurians* (1970), a prehistoric reptile civilisation has placed itself in suspended animation in subterranean caves in order to avoid an impending natural catastrophe. The arrival of a small planet prompted this action, but after they retreated into hibernation that satellite became the Moon. Thanks to a faulty hibernation mechanism, they're only awoken in the late 20th century by Wenley Moor's atomic reactor. The Silurians lie in individual sealed caskets and are revived by means of pulsing lights and heat, deriving energy from the research centre. Their marine cousins are awoken in *The Sea Devils* (1972). In *The Hungry Earth/Cold Blood* (2010), set in 2020, the reanimation of an entire city of Silurians is triggered by drilling from a scientific mining operation in Wales. Both Silurians and Sea Devils feature in *Warriors of the Deep* (1984), set in 2084. Here, groups of Sea Devil warriors are preserved in low temperature fluid within sealed cave chambers.

In *The Ark* (1966), we find the human race making its own plans to avoid impending catastrophe – this time using storage processes to allow for deep space travel. In the 57th Segment of Time, ten million years into the future, they flee their sun going supernova for a 700-year journey to Refusis II. The ship contains the Earth's entire population, reduced to microcell size and stored in trays in cabinets. (Again, see *Miniaturisation*, pages 52-55.) The United Earth colonists in *Smile* (2017) are also long-distance

SUSPENDING DISBELIEF

I n fairy stories, Sleeping Beauty and Snow White are placed in perpetual, unbreakable sleep states via magic. One of the first published fantasy tales to feature a similarly prolonged sleep was Washington Irving's *Rip Van Winkle* (1819), while one of science fiction's most famous 'sleepers', Buck Rogers, first appeared in the pulp magazine *Amazing Stories* in 1928.

Trapped in a cave and affected by radioactive gases, Rogers wakes up 500 years later in a space-age future. In the BBC television series *Adam Adamant Lives!* (1966-67), a Victorian gentleman adventurer is brought to swinging 1966, having been frozen in ice by his arch enemy. Mike Myers' satirical *Austin Powers* movies (1997-2002) feature a British secret agent cryogenically frozen in the late 1960s, waking 30 years later to lampoon the attitudes of an earlier generation. In *Alien* (1979), the Weyland Corporation's spaceships are equipped with 'hypersleep' chambers, while Dave Lister from the sci-fi sitcom *Red Dwarf* (1988-present) survives a radiation leak having been in stasis for three million years.

In one of the world's most persistent urban myths, many believe that the legendary animator and producer Walt Disney (among whose films were adaptations of the Snow White and Sleeping Beauty stories) had been cryogenically frozen in liquid nitrogen after his death from lung cancer in 1966, hoping to be revived years later when a cure might be found. In fact, Disney was cremated.

travellers, using suspended animation chambers on their ship, *Erehwon*, for their journey to the colony world Gliese 581 D.

Even small, one-man Arcatenian ships are equipped with a suspended animation chamber for long-haul flights. In *Under the Lake* (2015) a Tivolian undertaker has used an Arcatenian vessel to carry their tyrannical invader, the Fisher King, to his burial place. When the Doctor and Clara land on board underwater mining facility The Drum in 2119, they find the empty hearse ship and recover the seemingly occupied but deadlocked cryogenic chamber from the bottom of a lake. Then, in *Before the Flood* (2015), the Doctor travels back to 1980 to thwart the Fisher King's plans to place himself in suspended animation. After defeating him, the Doctor, without access to the TARDIS, locks himself in the suspended animation chamber. When it's reactivated 139 years later on The Drum, the Doctor is revealed to have been inside all along.

Another example of the human species avoiding imminent catastrophe is seen in *The Ark in Space* (1975). Here we find that solar flares destroyed life on Earth, with a few hundred survivors placed in suspended animation aboard the orbiting former space beacon Nerva. Selected from volunteers by the world executive, this cross-matched genetic pool was stored alongside animal and botanical specimens. Though the Earth was expected to be habitable again after 5,000 years, sabotage by a parasitic Wirrn queen has caused the Ark's inhabitants to oversleep by several thousand years.

Nerva's cryogenic process uses short-range matter transmitters to transport volunteers from a 'tranquiller' couch to the preparation unit, to the upright cryogenic pallet. After five minutes of biocryonic vibrations, volunteers undergo tissue irradiation, with the whole automated process taking well under an hour. The resuscitation phase is programmed in, with revivification aided by an injection to the heart of anti-protonic treatments. The vertically stacked pallets are arranged in pair-bonded couples, including the station's Commander Lazar (given the nickname Noah) and Vira. The Doctor points out that the cryogenic chambers are an old principle but have never, in his experience, been applied on such a scale.

S uspended animation can be applied on an individual level too. In *Destiny of the Daleks* (1979), Davros revives several centuries after the Daleks supposedly exterminated him. His chair's back-up systems assisted the process of synthetic tissue regeneration, while bodily organs were held in long-term suspension. Ironically, Davros is later placed in a cryogenic freezer on the trip back to Earth to face trial. Frozen, post-trial, inside a large cryogenic chamber aboard a space prison ship and held for 90 years, he's subsequently rescued by Lytton's troops in *Resurrection of the Daleks* (1984); as an apparent punishment, Davros remained conscious throughout.

Similar living deaths are visited upon those seeking Rassilon's secret of immortality in *The Five Doctors* (1983) – trapped, fully conscious, within carvings on Rassilon's tomb. Sutekh suffers a similar agonising punishment when bound by an Osiran forcefield for 7,000 years in *Pyramids of Mars* (1975).

Suspended animation is often suggested as the solution to terminal illness, with dying patients frozen until cures can be found. In *Revelation of the Daleks* (1985), Tranquil Repose holds a few thousand 'residents' in cryogenic caskets in the hope of later cures. It's implied their minds remain active, with their resting consciousnesses regularly updated by broadcasts from a relentlessly cheerful DJ. Davros, however, corrupts Tranquil Repose's function, using the bodies of the ambitious and powerful 'deceased' for Dalek experimentation and the rest as a lucrative foodstuff.

In *A Christmas Carol* (2010), Abigail Pettigrew is a young woman frozen for decades as security against a debt owed by her family to Elliot Sardick, a ruthless businessman. Sardick's basement vault, built on a lake of ice fog, contains hundreds of 'ice boxes' holding his debtors' family members. When the Doctor attempts to change history by making Sardick's bitter and ruthless son, Kazran, into a better person, he travels back to Kazran's childhood. It transpires that it was only after young Kazran fell in love with Abigail that he discovered she had been near death when she entered cryogenic sleep; with Abigail having just one day to live, Kazran has waited his whole lifetime to open the casket one final time.

A tragic twist on an age-old theme. ✸

Above: Davros (David Gooderson) is frozen at the end of *Destiny of the Daleks* (1979).

Left: Harry (Ian Marter), Vira (Wendy Williams) and the Doctor (Tom Baker) alongside some of the suspended animation chambers in *The Ark in Space* (1975).

TELEPORTATION

The technology is more closely associated with *Star Trek*, but the selective reassembling of atoms has loomed large in *Doctor Who*...

FEATURE BY **OLIVER WAKE**

The word 'teleport' was coined by Charles Fort in 1931, drawing on the Greek 'tele' (meaning 'far-off' or 'distant') and the Latin verb 'portare' (to carry). It refers to the movement of people or objects between two points, seemingly without traversing the distance between them. In *Doctor Who* it tends to be an instant or near-instant process accomplished by a variety of unlikely sciences, and it's known by a number of names. Numerous instances of teleportation can be seen in the series, so here we'll look at just a handful of the most notable examples of teleport technology and its applications.

Teleportation is introduced to *Doctor Who* very casually in Terry Nation's *The Keys of Marinus* (1964). The Doctor and his friends are transported around Marinus with wristwatch-like travel-dials given to them by Arbitan. There is no suggestion as to how they work, and though conveniently requiring no more technology than can be worn on the wrist, they are pre-programmed, giving the user no control over their destination.

Nation returns to teleportation in *The Daleks' Master Plan* (1965-66), when the Doctor, Steven and Sara are accidentally caught up in a human experiment in molecular dissemination in the year 4000. "To put it in lay language," says the Doctor, "cellular dissemination means our bodies were broken up by some process or other, shot through into the fourth dimension, and, at a given point, reassembled again on this planet." They find themselves on Mira, many light years from Earth. The process looks to be painful and renders them unconscious, although the laboratory mice who travel with them appear unperturbed.

It seems humanity has a long track record of experimental teleportation. In *The Time Monster* (1972) British scientists, sometime around the 1970s, are working on TOMTIT: Transmission of Matter Through Interstitial Time. This involves breaking down an object, as the Doctor helpfully puts it, "into light-waves or

TELEPORTATION IS INTRODUCED TO *DOCTOR WHO* VERY CASUALLY IN TERRY NATION'S *THE KEYS OF MARINUS*.

whatever," pushing these through the interstices between temporal atoms into 'nowhere', before reassembling them where desired. The team succeeds in moving a vase several feet, but it transpires the Master is behind the process and using it for evil ends. Unsurprisingly, it takes humanity much longer to develop a more effective version of the technology.

Humans have another go in the early 21st century, with UNIT's Project Indigo, seen in *The Stolen Earth/Journey's End* (2008). Indigo is an experimental teleport backpack salvaged from the Sontarans. It's used by Martha Jones but, without co-ordinates or stabilisation, Captain Jack Harkness anticipates her atoms will simply be scattered. He's proved wrong, with Martha ▶

Mat.Ac.Stage I.

Opposite page: Martha Jones (Freema Agyeman) uses Project Indigo, an early teleport device, in *The Stolen Earth/Journey's End* (2008).

Left: Dr Ruth Ingram (Wanda Moore) at the controls of TOMTIT in *The Time Monster* (1972).

Top: Ian (William Russell), the Doctor (William Hartnell) and Susan (Carole Ann Ford) use travel dials in *The Keys of Marinus* (1964).

Above: Sara Kingdom (Jean Marsh) teleports in *The Daleks' Master Plan* (1965-66).

Above left: Jamie (Frazer Hines), the Doctor (Patrick Troughton) and Zoe (Wendy Padbury) travel by T-Mat in *The Seeds of Death* (1969).

Above right: 'Edgeworth' (Maurice Denham) by the revitalising modulator in *The Twin Dilemma* (1984).

Below: Gia Kelly (Louise Pajo) in *The Seeds of Death*.

Below right: Sarah (Elisabeth Sladen), the Doctor (Tom Baker) and Harry (Ian Marter) arrive by time ring in *Revenge of the Cybermen* (1975).

◀ speculating that perhaps some psychic link selected the correct destination. With access to the teleport base code, the system is made reliable.

By the time of *The Seeds of Death* (1969), not only does humanity have fully functional teleportation technology but Earth has become entirely reliant upon it for its transport needs. Travel-Mat, or T-Mat, beams people and supplies by microwave between reception centres on Earth, via a pivotal control centre on the Moon. The Moonbase can handle two million microwave channels simultaneously, but with the Moon relay out of action a satellite could carry a few thousand channels as an emergency backup. The Doctor expects a T-Mat journey to be fun but finds it "rather disappointing – there's no sensation at all". T-Mat predates the experimental teleportation of *The Daleks' Master Plan*, but in the latter the scientists seem to be working on a system designed primarily for ultra-long-range usage, whereas T-Mat serves the Earth and the Moon only.

Later, *Doctor Who* discovered new narrative possibilities of teleportation science, beyond straightforward travel.

In *Revenge of the Cybermen* (1975), the Doctor finds a matter transmitter (or 'transmat' for short) a convenient method of curing Sarah Jane Smith when she's poisoned by a Cybermat. "The matter beam disperses human molecules," says the Doctor. "That type of alien poison might be separated and rejected." It works, and fortunately the transmat *doesn't* reject the animal and synthetic molecules of her clothing! *The Pirate Planet* (1978) gives us the most extreme example of teleportation in the series, with "vast transmat engines" used to drop the hollow planet Zanak "out of the space dimension" and materialise it around other, smaller worlds.

EARTH HAS BECOME ENTIRELY RELIANT ON T-MAT FOR ITS TRANSPORT NEEDS.

In *The Twin Dilemma* (1984) we see a device that shares some intriguing similarities with a transmat. The Doctor reveals that it's a "revitalising modulator. It breaks down your molecular structure and puts it back together again. A most refreshing process." He's able to improvise additional functions, making it project and reassemble those molecules in the TARDIS (and adding a tiny degree of time travel), to enable his and Peri's escape from an exploding base.

The most intriguing questions around the science of teleportation concern the deconstruction of the subject's molecules; what would happen if their transmission stalled or was interrupted? "Don't you realise how dangerous it is to intercept a transmat beam?" asks the Doctor, when the Time Lords redirect his matter transmission in *Genesis of the Daleks* (1975).

More recent series of *Doctor Who* have run with the dramatic possibilities of unconventional teleportation usage. In Russell T Davies' *Voyage of the Damned* (2007), the space liner *Titanic* operates a teleport system to enable passengers

MIND OVER MATTER

Although teleportation is usually achieved via technological means, some species in *Doctor Who* are capable of teleporting themselves – or others – without any mechanical assistance. In *Planet of the Spiders* (1974), the giant spiders of Metebelis III harness their own mental powers to jump the vast distance between their world and Earth, through both time and space. The Sisterhood of Karn in *The Brain of Morbius* (1976) teleport the TARDIS and the Doctor into their shrine as a result of their combined chants of reverence for their sacred flame. It seems to be an ancient dark art, with the Doctor

remarking: "What, you mean you still practise teleportation? How quaint! Now, if you got yourself a decent forklift truck…"

One of the most mysterious applications of teleportation in *Doctor Who* is that of the alien parasite in *The Mind of Evil* (1971).

Presumably this is an innate ability of the creature when looking for victims to feed upon, and it seems to have only a short range. In *Survival* (1989), the Kitlings and Cheetah People can teleport themselves, and their victims, between other worlds and their own unnamed planet. This is a result of their symbiotic relationship with the living world. "Only the animals of this place can leave," says the Master, "because they carry it with them." But even visitors take on the ability to teleport as the planet starts to exerts its influence over them, though the infection and teleport ability passes when they leave.

to visit nearby planets. It has emergency fail-safes, according to Mr Copper: "If a passenger has an accident on shore leave and they're still wearing their teleport [bracelet], their molecules are automatically suspended and held in stasis." In effect, the teleporter records a 'backup' of the subject. He's able to recall Astrid Peth, who has recently died while wearing her teleport bracelet, but only as a temporary, partial manifestation: "The system is too badly damaged. She's just atoms, Doctor. An echo with the ghost of consciousness. She's stardust."

Writer Steven Moffat has revisited this idea twice, suggesting that the disassembled molecules of a teleportation subject are little different from computer data and can be stored as such. In

Silence in the Library/Forest of the Dead (2008), we learn how a teleporter caused over 4,000 people to go missing. When an alarm was activated, the Library's computer tried to protect all of its users. "It succeeded," says the Doctor. "Pulled them all out, but then what? Nowhere to send them. Nowhere safe in the whole library. Vashta Nerada growing in every shadow. Four thousand and twenty-two people all beamed up and nowhere to go. They're stuck in the system, waiting to be sent, like emails… The computer saved four thousand and twenty-two people the only way a computer can. It saved them to the hard drive."

When the Vashta Nerada depart, the missing people are reconstituted from their stored energy signatures.

In Moffat's *Heaven Sent* (2015), the Doctor is able to spend four-and-a-half billion years (and many more lives) escaping from the confession dial prison thanks to the "augmented ultra-long-range teleport" he arrived by and

Above left: Tourists from the *Titanic* visit London in *Voyage of the Damned* (2007).

Left inset: Astrid (Kylie Minogue) becomes stardust in *Voyage of the Damned.*

Below left: The computer CAL in *Silence in the Library/Forest of the Dead* (2008).

Below right: The Doctor (Peter Capaldi) in *Heaven Sent* (2015).

the prison's regularly resetting rooms. Each lifetime he makes slight progress in eroding the harder-than-diamond Azbantium that blocks his exit, before being killed. He describes his plan: "Teleporter. Fancy word. Just like 3D printers really, except they break down living matter and information, and transmit it… The room has reset, returned to its original condition when I arrived. That means there's a copy of me still in the hard drive. Me, exactly as I was, when I first got here." He just needs an energy source, for which he supplies himself, burning, and the teleporter generates a new copy of him replacing the recently dead one. Eventually, after billions of repetitions, the Doctor breaks through the Azbantium to freedom.

The use of teleportation in *Voyage of the Damned, Silence in the Library/Forest of the Dead* and *Heaven Sent* raises an intriguing question. If a teleporter can store a person as little more than data, and potentially reconstitute them only after a lengthy passage of time (a hundred years in the case of the Library's unlucky users), or in many identical iterations as in *Heaven Sent*, is the person who comes out of the teleporter really the same person who went in…? ⚛

THE TIME LORDS

Of all the technology in the universe, none is more impressive than that created by the Doctor's own people...

FEATURE BY **JOHN J JOHNSTON**

For many millions of years, the Time Lords of Gallifrey have held a preeminent position in the universe as a race of tremendous scientific knowledge and technological ability. Their relationship with technology is, however, highly complex...

Gallifrey's technological zenith appears to have been in its ancient past, when the planet's scientific ascendancy was ensured by the solar researches of the pioneering engineer Omega. Creating a supernova by means of a remote stellar manipulator (ostentatiously, though perhaps unsurprisingly, named the Hand of Omega), he provided his people with an enormous power source and made their proposed time experiments a reality.

In *Remembrance of the Daleks* (1988) it's revealed that the Doctor has hidden the Hand of Omega in 1963 London. The device is a large, tarnished, metallic sarcophagus structure, with a low degree of sentience but capable of autonomous movement and able to respond to the Doctor's verbal instructions. In addition to destroying Skaro's sun, the Hand is capable of bestowing, through undisclosed means, increased strength and hitherto unrealised destructive properties upon an unremarkable baseball bat.

Following the apparent demise of Omega in the conflagration resulting from the Hand's original detonation, the earliest Time Lords misused their burgeoning technological powers disgracefully. Their Time Scoop was capable of gathering groups and individuals from across time and space and depositing them in Gallifrey's 'Death Zone'. In this damp and inhospitable terrain, enclosed within a largely impenetrable force field, 'lesser species' were forced to engage in gladiatorial combat for the amusement of the nascent Time Lord culture.

This obscene practise was apparently ended by Rassilon. Though primarily an engineer and an architect, his influence on political and social matters encouraged later Time Lords to view him as the true founder of their society. Rassilon refined and perfected Omega's initial scientific developments by stabilising all the elements of a black hole and setting them in an eternally dynamic equation against the mass of the planet – thus creating the Eye of Harmony, from which all the power of the Time Lords, from time travel to regeneration, would derive.

During this period the Time Lords sought to protect themselves by designing ever greater weapons of enormous destructive power. The living, sentient metal validium, originated by Omega and finessed by Rassilon, could be fashioned into any form and accidentally arrived on Earth in 17th-century Windsor. Although the Doctor succeeded in launching the material back into space (in a continuous 25-year orbit around the Earth), its baleful influence nevertheless had ▶

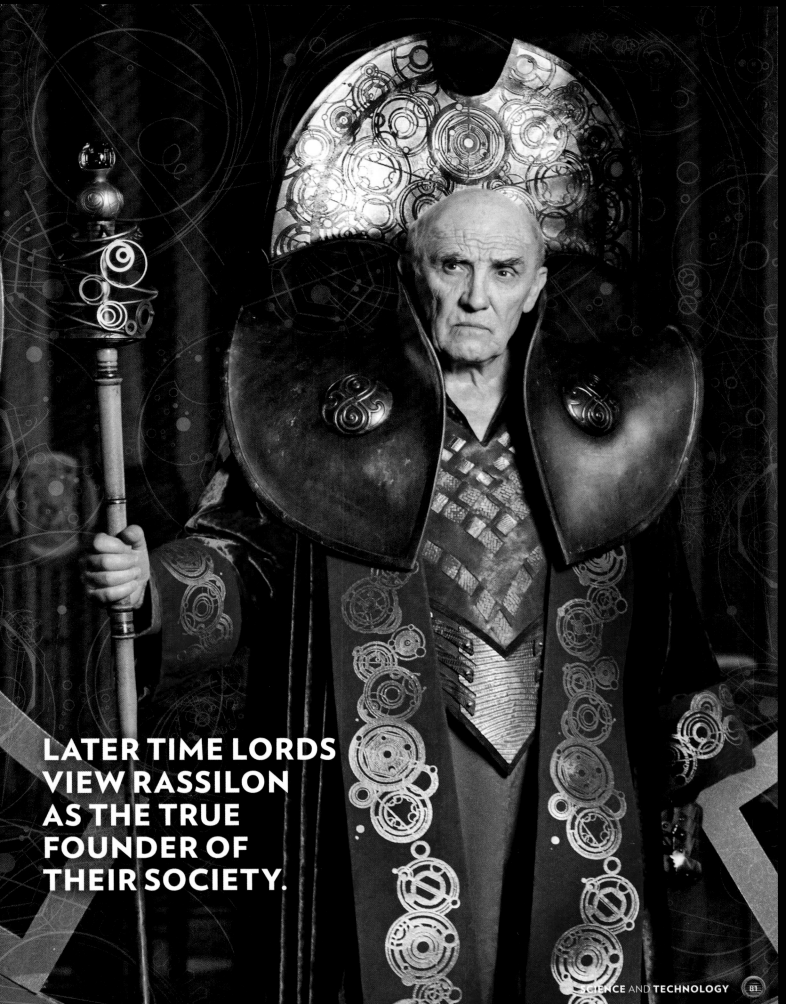

LATER TIME LORDS VIEW RASSILON AS THE TRUE FOUNDER OF THEIR SOCIETY.

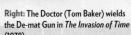

Right: The Doctor (Tom Baker) wields the De-mat Gun in *The Invasion of Time* (1978).

Far right: The Doctor (John Hurt) contemplates using the Moment in *The Day of the Doctor*.

Right inset: Gallifreyan symbols from *The Day of the Doctor*.

Below: The Doctor (Matt Smith) uses artron energy to swap bodies with Clyde in *The Death of the Doctor*, a 2010 episode of *The Sarah Jane Adventures*.

Bottom: The Daleks' Genesis Ark is primed by artron energy from Mickey Smith (Noel Clarke) in *Doomsday* (2006).

◀ a catastrophic effect on Earth events. Though largely passive, the validium, fashioned into a statue of Jacobean sorceress Lady Peinforte and given the name Nemesis, was capable of full conversational interaction, including the disclosure of secrets from Gallifrey's ancient past.

In *The Invasion of Time* (1978) we encounter the De-mat Gun, originally conceived by Rassilon and capable of entirely dematerialising any target. The Doctor views it as the ultimate weapon, capable of wiping out the Sontaran invasion force on Gallifrey. Lord Chancellor Borusa is horrified that a firearm of such destructive force has been recreated, believing that it could send Time Lord society back to the dark ages.

The last and arguably the most destructive of the ancient Gallifreyan weapons, known as the Moment and colloquially referred to as 'the galaxy eater', was so immensely powerful that its sentient interface developed a conscience, capable of dissuading potential operators from triggering the weapon. The Moment initially had the physical form of a square, medium-sized wooden box with an intricate clockwork mechanism, prefiguring the Time Lord confession dial first seen in *The Magician's Apprentice* (2015). This was replaced with a more familiar big red button, satisfying the Doctor's aesthetic sense. As the interface has the ability to assume a recognisable appearance – taking the form, in the 2005 story *Bad Wolf*, of Rose Tyler's 'Bad Wolf' persona – the Moment adopts an ornately vegetable appearance atop a plinth, with a large, multifaceted red gemstone surrounded by brass sepals.

It seems that, beyond time travel, the ancient Time Lords' vast technological proficiency took two very specific directions: the development of impenetrable defences together with vast and diabolical weaponry. Both of these exemplify the Time Lords' distinctly xenophobic view of the universe and their more immediate topographical environment.

ARTRON ENERGY

Artron energy is a naturally occurring phenomenon which is directly connected to the practise of travelling through the Time Vortex. All Time Lords are affected by it to some degree, and it's possible that noviciates first encounter the energy when they're introduced to Gallifrey's Untempered Schism at the commencement of their training.

The energy accretes to TARDIS time capsules and to their inhabitants, and is recognised as an essentially beneficial side effect of time travel; the Doctor's considerable resilience has been attributed to his substantial reserves of artron energy, undoubtedly due to his frequent exposure to the Vortex. In utero exposure to artron energy is almost certainly responsible for River Song's peculiarly Time Lord nature, in spite of both parents hailing from Earth. Towards the end of the Time War, the Daleks turned

contact with their Time Lord enemies into a means of personal regeneration, as with Van Statten's prized extra-terrestrial exhibit in *Dalek* (2005). In a similar manner, artron energy reactivates the Time Lord prison, described by the Daleks as the 'Genesis Ark'.

Artron energy has also been described as TARDIS power (in *The Sarah Jane Adventures: The Wedding of Sarah Jane*, 2009) and its scent is detectable by certain species, such as the Groske in *The Sarah Jane Adventures: The Death of the Doctor* (2010). In addition, artron energy allowed UNIT to detect the arrival of the Doctor's TARDIS at Amy and Rory's home in *The Power of Three* (2012).

onsequently – in addition to a series of transduction barriers, intended to prevent the materialisation of unauthorised TARDIS time capsules within the Capitol – Gallifrey is also protected by a vast quantum force field. This was devised by Rassilon and can't be fully dismantled without the possibility of the planet being vaporised.

The Time Lord Capitol is sheltered among, and from, Gallifrey's mountains of Solace and Solitude by a gigantic, transparent dome resembling a vast snow-globe. There appears to be no obvious reason for this structure. Although Gallifrey is evidently something of a desert, it's certainly not inimical to humanoid life, and Gallifrey's second city, Arcadia, appears to have no such dome. Time Lords can enter and depart the Capitol with comparative freedom, so it seems likely that this protective dome is more an immense statement of technological prowess and perpetual vigilance – in addition to providing a magnificent setting for the centre of Time Lord life.

During the Time War, Gallifrey's defences were further augmented by a series of sky trenches, possibly also created by Rassilon, who, following his resurrection, had joined battle anew. These linear aerial force fields protected major cities from attack from above, in the same fashion as the trenches of World War I prevented troops from easily negotiating terrestrial battlefields. Nothing had successfully penetrated more than two of the sky trenches until the final day of the Time War, and the Daleks' devastation of Arcadia.

Curiously, the Time Lords' memory of Rassilon and his technological achievements diminished significantly during the millennia following his death. The Book of the Old Time swathed his considerable accomplishments in a mytho-religious narrative, appealing to the Time Lords' view of their position within the universe as immensely powerful beings transcending the boundaries of technology.

Indeed, the Time Lords' first appearance in *Doctor Who* presents them as beings of almost god-like capability. At the conclusion of *The War Games* (1969), their use of time technology allows them to place the unnamed home world of the War Lord within a force field, imprisoning the inhabitants forever, while the War Lord and his bellicose associates are entirely removed from time, as if they had never existed. This appears a somewhat extreme and hypocritical stance, given that the War Lord's games were presumably inspired by the ancient games of the Death Zone, at the suggestion of the War Chief – himself a Time Lord.

The technology seen in this first appearance appears to be telepathically controlled by the three robed Time Lords administering the trials of both the War Lord and the Second Doctor; there's a very real sense that the technology at their disposal is an extension of their mental abilities.

Arguably, it's only when the Master leads an assault upon the Panopticon (in *The Deadly Assassin*, 1976) that the Time Lords fully appreciate the Eye of Harmony as a very real technological phenomenon and that their gilded lifestyles are, in fact, dependent upon scientific principles. The Eye itself is buried beneath the very hub of Gallifreyan political and ritual life, held in place by a tall, obelisk-like structure. ▶

Above: The Time Lords (Clyde Pollitt, Bernard Horsfall and Trevor Martin) seen in Episode Ten of *The War Games* (1969) appear to have god-like powers.

Left: The General (Ken Bones) and Androgar (Peter de Jersey) track the progress of the Time War in *The Day of the Doctor*.

Below: The Doctor is given a chance to change his mind when the Moment adopts the form of Rose Tyler's 'Bad Wolf' persona (Billie Piper).

THE MOMENT IS THE MOST DESTRUCTIVE OF THE ANCIENT GALLIFREYAN WEAPONS.

Above: Lord Rassilon (Timothy Dalton) chairs a meeting of the High Council in *The End of Time* (2009-10).

Above right: The General, backed up by his troops, attempts to talk to the Doctor in *Hell Bent* (2015).

Right inset: 'The Worshipful and Ancient Law of Gallifrey', as seen in the 2017 version of *Shada*.

Below left: The Doctor, in full Time Lord regalia, is recognised by Runcible (Hugh Walters) in *The Deadly Assassin*.

Below right: The Doctor confers with Engin (Erik Chitty) and Spandrell (George Pravda) in *The Deadly Assassin*.

◀ Physical deterrents to antisocial behaviour are, as might be expected, a vitally important technological element of Time Lord society. The standard weapon employed by the Chancery Guard is the staser, a particularly unpleasant energy firearm that can be set to stun but can also char the body beyond recognition within an hour.

Similarly, the distant prison planet of Shada, which may only be approached via 'The Worshipful and Ancient Law of Gallifrey', is a disagreeable deterrent for immensely long-lived miscreants, who may be incarcerated for millennia. Apparently a medium-sized, red-bound hardback book, the volume is, in fact, a technologically advanced key, without atomic structure and impervious to analysis or damage, capable of transporting the reader to Shada if utilised within a TARDIS.

Perhaps as a direct result of the Time Lords' elevated and hubristic attitude, their science has become inextricably linked with tradition and ritual. During *The Deadly Assassin* Engin, a senior Time Lord

THE TIME LORDS' ELEVATED SCIENCE HAS BECOME LINKED WITH TRADITION AND RITUAL.

technician, speaks of Gallifrey having "turned aside from the barren road of technology", while even the Fourth Doctor describes the assembled equipment as "prehistoric junk".

The Matrix is another remarkable example of the Time Lords' overweening desire for self-preservation. The virtual reality aspects of the Matrix are detailed on pages 104-09, but it's worth noting here certain physical elements of this vast repository of knowledge. The aforementioned Co-ordinator Engin operates the equipment required to upload the knowledge and personalities of Time Lords at the moment of their death – trillions of electrochemical cells in a continuous matrix – to the Amplified Panatropic Computations Net. This allows life within the Capitol to be monitored, thereby predicting future developments: a surprisingly imprudent course for a species capable of time travel.

Disturbingly, however, semi-corporeal versions of these deceased Time Lords continue to haunt the crypt-like cloisters as 'Cloister Wraiths', providing a security mechanism capable of neutralising potential physical threats to the Matrix. It's

THE **RELICS** OF **RASSILON**

A number of the artefacts of the Old Time are either attributed to Rassilon's invention or simply bear his name. Some are exhibited in a display vitrine in the Panopticon:

THE SASH
Essentially the President's ceremonial chain of office, worn around the neck. It was devised by Rassilon when he stabilised the Eye of Harmony and prevents the wearer from being drawn into a black hole.

THE ROD
Sometimes, erroneously, referred to as the Great Key. The rod is an ebonite sceptre carried by the president on ceremonial occasions. Its original function was to release, direct and control the tremendous forces held in check by the Eye of Harmony.

In addition to these relics on display, a number of other artefacts are known of, including:

THE CROWN
An outwardly bevelled gold diadem, inset with amber-coloured gemstones. It's set into the Panopticon dais and is worn only by the elected President of the Supreme (or High Council) of the Time Lords, allowing the wearer complete access to the Matrix. It is the most important element of the president's investiture.

THE GREAT KEY
A large but otherwise standard metal key. It is held, secretly, in trust by the chancellor in order to prevent the president from holding absolute power, for the Key may be used to arm the formidable De-mat gun.

THE HARP
Displayed in the Conference Chamber of the High Council. When correctly played, it allows access to the Time Scoop control room, discovered by Borusa in his quest for immortality.

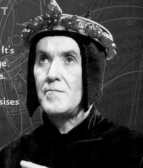

THE CORONET
A gold filigree diadem with a frontal rhombus. It's studded with large purple gemstones. Discovered by Borusa, it emphasises the wearer's will, controlling the minds of all in the vicinity.

a peculiarly nightmarish concept of the afterlife for individuals who have already contributed their substantial existences to the tedious ritual of Time Lord society.

There is, therefore, a very real sense that, having withdrawn behind their force fields as somewhat voyeuristic intergalactic observers, the Time Lords have become a decadent culture, entirely reliant upon their past scientific glories and content to play the role of Professor Marvel, somewhat impotently operating levers behind the curtain in their glittering Emerald City.

Although Time Lords are wont to boast of their technological accomplishments, particularly to the Doctor, there are surprising gaps in their knowledge and skills. According to *The Invasion of Time* (1978), the metal lead is deemed to be a very difficult substance to control, with only a few Time Lords having mastered the art. Artisanship is beyond, or perhaps beneath the dignity of the Time Lords, with artwork being created either by computer or through the use of stasis cubes; these appear to be highly detailed, three-dimensional renderings but are, in fact, slices of real time, held in stasis within a frame. The most notable example is *Gallifrey Falls No More*, held in the National Gallery in *The Day of the Doctor* (2013).

Although TARDIS time capsules are the most frequently utilised method of travelling beyond Gallifrey, the Time Lords have developed a smaller portable device, the time ring, which may be worn on the wrist and will transport an individual and a small number of companions back to a preordained location – most frequently either Gallifrey or to a TARDIS. It's likely, given their size and aptitude for covert usage, that

these are primarily employed by operatives of the Celestial Intervention Agency. The technology appears similar to both the Stattenheim Remote Control (which may be used, in particular circumstances, by TARDIS pilots) and to Vortex manipulators used by time agents of the 51st century.

In the opening moments of *Genesis of the Daleks* (1975) a puzzled Doctor is told that "We Time Lords transcended such simple mechanical devices when the universe was less than half its present size." In *The End of Time* (2009-10) Rassilon reveals his ambition for the Time Lords to divest their corporeal form and become creatures of consciousness. The Doctor thwarts this plan, but this doesn't rule out the possibility that Time Lord technology may one day become truly indistinguishable from magic.

Clockwise from top left: The relics of Rassilon – The Doctor is presented with the Sash, and then the Crown by Gold Usher (Charles Morgan) in *The Invasion of Time*; the Doctor (Peter Davison) inspects the Harp in *The Five Doctors* (1983); Borusa (Philip Latham) wears the Coronet in *The Five Doctors*; the Great Key from *The Invasion of Time*, and the Rod from *The Invasion of Time*.

Below: The Doctors (David Tennant and Matt Smith) study *Gallifrey Falls No More* in *The Day of the Doctor*.

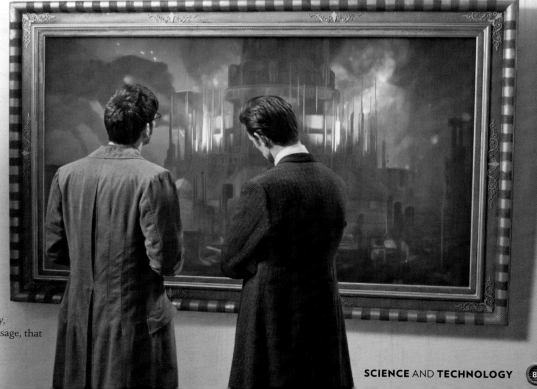

TIME TRAVEL

The most powerful technology in the universe is one that has been mastered by the Doctor's own people, and attempted by many others...

FEATURE BY **STEVE LYONS**

"Time travel is damage," says the Doctor in *The Name of the Doctor* (2013). "It's like a tear in the fabric of reality."

Specifically, time travel means traversing the Space-Time Vortex, an extra-temporal plane that links all times and places. We see it in one of its varied forms in the very first episode, *An Unearthly Child* (1963), but it isn't until 1972's *Day of the Daleks* that it's given a name – by a Dalek, of all creatures.

From this point on, it's variously referred to as 'the Time Vortex', 'the Time-Space Vortex' or simply 'the Vortex', a realm where (in *The Time Monster*, 1972) 'E=MC^3'. To complicate matters, it's often suggested that there's more than one vortex, although each of these appears to be a subset of *the* Vortex...

The mere sight of the Vortex is enough to cause insanity, according to *The Sound of Drums* (2007). Exposure to it leaves one charged with artron energy; first named in 1976's *The Deadly Assassin*, this effect was spelled out in 2007's *The Sarah Jane Adventures: Invasion of the Bane*. It was this that, over billions of years, turned the people of Gallifrey into Time Lords (*A Good Man Goes to War*, 2011).

The Gallifreyans were the first to discover (or maybe even create) the Vortex, and to harness the tremendous amount of power required to access it. This enabled them to develop

TIME TRAVEL MEANS TRAVERSING THE SPACE-TIME VORTEX, AN EXTRA-TEMPORAL PLANE THAT LINKS ALL TIMES AND PLACES.

such useful devices as the time scoop (*The Five Doctors*, 1983), which can pluck any being out of history; chronodyne generators or time mines to blast their enemies into the future (*The Caretaker*, 2014); and the time ring – a personal Vortex travel device first seen in *Genesis of the Daleks* (1975).

Time travel without a capsule, however, is "nasty" according to the Doctor in *Blink* (2007). Hence the Time Lords' crowning achievement is the TARDIS: a time-space vehicle fitted with a Vortex drive (*Delta and the Bannermen*, 1987), allowing it – if we believe the Doctor – to *tear* its way into and out of that realm. The materialisation of a TARDIS is described by the Captain, in 1978's *The Pirate Planet*, thus: "For ten seconds, the entire fabric of the space-time continuum was ripped apart."

The Time Lords guard their secrets jealously. In *The Time Warrior* (1973-74) the Doctor claims that they're "very keen to stamp out unlicensed time travel." They can't plug every leak, however.

In *The War Games* (1969), for example, the War Lord, leader of an unknown alien race, kidnaps Earthlings from historical war zones to create an all-conquering army. A renegade Time Lord, the War Chief, constructs SIDRATs – cut-price TARDISes with shorter life spans – to assist him. Third Zone scientists Kartz and Reimer copy Time Lord technology to build a transference module in *The Two Doctors* (1985), successfully sending test subjects into the time stream but killing ►

Left: The Vortex, seen through the Untempered Schism in *The Sound of Drums* (2007).

Left inset: Seeing the Vortex had a profound effect on the eight-year-old Master (William Hughes) in *The Sound of Drums*.

Below left: Zoe (Wendy Padbury) and the Doctor (Patrick Troughton) aboard a SIDRAT in *The War Games* (1969).

Below: Group Marshal Stike (Clinton Greyn) is seriously injured in his attempt to travel through time in *The Two Doctors* (1985).

Right: Craig (James Corden) and the Doctor (Matt Smith) discover an abandoned time-travelling vessel in *The Lodger* (2010).

Far right: Lady Peinforte (Fiona Walker) appears to use magic to travel forward in time in *Silver Nemesis* (1988).

Below centre: Donna Noble (Catherine Tate) prepares to travel back in time...

Below left: ...and realises that she has a Time Beetle on her back in *Turn Left* (2008).

Below right: An android (Dean Hollingsworth) pushes another victim into the *Timelash* (1985).

◀ them in the process thanks to their lack of a molecular stabilisation system. Time Lords may have been implanted with symbiotic nuclei for just this purpose – or the Doctor may have fabricated this claim for the benefit of an eavesdropping Sontaran. The Cybermen, too, possess stolen time travel – briefly – after capturing a time vessel of unknown origin in *Attack of the Cybermen* (1985).

Other races have developed time travel by their own efforts. The inventors of the Miniscope incorporate something like a time scoop into its workings in *Carnival of Monsters* (1973) and Sontarans can send themselves a few centuries into the future with an osmic projector, according to *The Time Warrior*. Meglos, the last Zolfa-Thuran, is knowledgeable enough to trap the Doctor in a time loop, or chronic hysteresis (*Meglos*, 1980), while in *Terminus* (1983) we're told by the Doctor that the titular space station "was once capable of time travel".

The Silents have time-travelling ships, which the Doctor describes – upon finding an abandoned one – as "someone's attempt to build a TARDIS" (*The Lodger*, 2010). Androzani trees can actually grow Vortex-traversing vessels; they require a strong female mind, however – along with a mechanical relay – to pilot them (*The Doctor, the Widow and the Wardrobe*, 2011).

EARTH'S FIRST TIME-TRAVELLER MAY HAVE BEEN LADY PEINFORTE. IN *SILVER NEMESIS*. SHE LEAPS FORWARD 350 YEARS FROM 1638.

The ancient Osirans, the Karfelian scientist the Borad and the 51st-century repair droids of the *SS Madame de Pompadour* have all constructed tunnels through the Vortex, linking two fixed points. An Osiran time-space tunnel acts as a lodestone to the Doctor's TARDIS in 1975's *Pyramids of Mars*. Such tunnels, however, age (or presumably de-age) the traveller proportionately, thus allowing travel only within one's lifetime. In *Timelash* (1985), the Borad's tunnel runs in one direction only, so he doesn't know where it terminates. He christens it "the Timelash" and banishes political dissidents into it – to 12th-century Scotland, as it happens.

The Timelash may be powered by time-distorting kontron crystals – or they may grow inside the Vortex; this isn't made clear. The 'time windows' of the Clockwork Droids, on the other hand, are powered by their ship's warp engines. In *Twice Upon a Time* (2017), Professor Helen Clay of the University

SIDEWAYS IN TIME

Not all time travel is forwards or backwards. In 1970's *Inferno*, for example, an attempt to repair the TARDIS sends the Doctor sideways in time to a parallel Earth. When a similar mishap occurs in 2006's *Rise of the Cybermen*, he clarifies (in the following episode, *Age of Steel*) that ordinarily this would be impossible, unless they fell through a crack in time.

A Time Beetle creates a parallel world around Donna Noble by altering her past (*Turn Left*, 2008). In this world, the Doctor dies circa 2006 and UNIT gains possession of his TARDIS. Unable to fathom its finer workings, they cannibalise it to build a rudimentary time machine. This machine – or maybe just a central component of it – is christened 'the lodestone', suggesting

the influence of Osiran technology. The user wears a special jacket as insulation against temporal feedback. A circle of mirrors is also employed (recalling Maxtible and Waterfield's experiment in *The Evil of the Daleks*) – though, according to Rose Tyler, "the mirrors are just incidental. They bounce chronon energy back into the centre, which we control and decide the destination."

of New Earth established the Testimony Foundation in the year 5,000,000,012. Its purpose is to lift the near-dead from their time streams and duplicate their memories.

Earth's first time-traveller may have been Lady Peinforte. In *Silver Nemesis* (1988), she leaps forward 350 years from 1638, allegedly by black magic – although the Doctor later intimates in *The Curse of Fenric* (1989) that the evil force, Fenric, may have had a hand in this feat. The first scientific breakthrough in the field occurred in 1866 – when Theodore Maxtible concocted a theory involving mirrors, electromagnetism and static electricity. In 1967's *The Evil of the Daleks*, he funds and works

with Edward Waterfield to prove it.

"A mirror reflects an image, does it not?" he explains. "Waterfield and I first attempted to refine the image in the mirror and then to project it." They fit out a cabinet with 144 mirrors, made of polished metal and statically charged. Improbable as it seems, their experiment meets with partial success, in that it provides the Daleks with access to the 19th century.

A Professor Whitaker constructs a working time scoop and brings dinosaurs to the present day in *Invasion of the Dinosaurs* (1974). By a "different application of the same basic principle" he then *reverses* time in a localised field, intending to roll back time across Earth itself, returning it to "an earlier, purer age". Whether it would have worked or not, we'll never know. The Doctor reverses the machine's polarity, hurling Whitaker and his associate into the distant past.

In *City of Death* (1979), Professor Theodor Nickolai Kerensky is working along similar lines but to a different end. His goal is to build a cellular accelerator, which will end famine by speeding the growth of food animals within a time bubble. The Doctor is scornful: "You can stretch time backwards or forwards within that bubble, but you can't break into it or out of it."

Kerensky doesn't know that his work is funded by an alien being. Like Professor Whitaker, Scaroth – the last of the Jagaroth – plots to expand Kerensky's bubble around ▶

Above centre: Professor Kerensky (David Graham) conducts experiments with time...

Above left: ... in a very high-tech laboratory in *City of Death* (1979).

Above right: Theodore Maxtible (Marius Goring) experimented with time travel in *The Evil of the Daleks* (1967).

Below left: Butler (Martin Jarvis) and Captain Mike Yates (Richard Franklin) watch as Professor Whitaker moves prehistoric creatures into the present day in *Invasion of the Dinosaurs* (1974)...

Below right: ... including this Triceratops in the London Underground.

Above left: Orson Pink (Samuel Anderson) is stranded at the end of the universe in *Listen* (2014).

Above right: The Doctor rescues Hila Tacorien (Kemi-Bo Jacobs) from being trapped in a pocket universe in *Hide* (2013).

Right inset: Heather (Stepahnie Hyam) appears to have innate time-travelling abilities in *The Pilot* (2017).

Below: Captain Jack Harness (John Barrowman) wears a Vortex manipulator on his wrist in *The Doctor Dances* (2005).

the world, reversing time to the point where he can change the fate of his extinct race. Unexpectedly, however, he acquires a field interface stabiliser from the Time Lord Romana. With this technology, he steps into Kerensky's bubble and travels back in time himself – albeit, temporarily.

Maxtible, Waterfield, Whitaker and Kerensky all perish before publishing their findings. Only in the early years of the 22nd century does the age of human time travel really begin. Orson Pink claims that time travel "runs in the family", and we're told by the Doctor that Pink "rode the first of the great time shots"; the intention was to send himself one week forward in time, but he overshot and became stranded "at the end of time itself" (*Listen*, 2014). Another of this era's pioneers, Hila Tacorien, was stuck in a pocket universe for billions of years – or, from her point of view, a few minutes (*Hide*, 2013). The Doctor is able to take Pink home but not Tacorien – implying that her contribution to posterity will be more significant.

Nearly 3,000 years after these early setbacks – a hiatus the Doctor blames on "Findecker's discovery of the double-nexus particle, [which] sent human science up a technological cul-de-sac" – the 51st-century war criminal Magnus Greel steals an experimental time cabinet and flees to 19th-century China, becoming, he believes, "the first man to travel through time". The cabinet, based

TIME AGENTS ARE ISSUED WITH VORTEX MANIPULATORS: WRIST-WORN DEVICES FIRST SEEN IN JACK'S POSSESSION IN *THE EMPTY CHILD*.

on Findecker's principles, is powered by a beam of zygma energy but ravages the user's DNA. Even worse, a single journey leaves the zygma beam at full stretch. A second will mean "certain collapse... a huge implosion" (*The Talons of Weng-Chiang*, 1977).

Curiously, Greel expresses concern that a Time Agent may come after him. This implies knowledge of the Time Agency: a mysterious organisation also active in the early 5000s. Captains Jack Harkness (first seen in 2005's *The Empty Child*) is a Time Agent, undermining Greel's "first man" boast – unless he meant "first Earth-born man".

Time Agents are issued with Vortex manipulators: wrist-worn devices first seen in Jack's possession in *The Empty Child*, with their name and function only revealed in 2007's *Utopia*. "That's not time travel," scoffs the Doctor. "It's like, I've got a sports car and you've got a space hopper."

River Song is more appreciative. She buys her device, still attached to a Time Agent's wrist, in *The Pandorica Opens* (2010). "Less bulky than a TARDIS," she says in 2012's *The Angels Take Manhattan*. "A motorbike through traffic." Either way, they do the job. A stolen manipulator allows the Family of Blood to follow the TARDIS wherever they go across the universe in *Human Nature* (2007).

Other beings appear to have innate time-travelling abilities. These include Fenric, the Eternals (*Enlightenment*, 1983) and human beings merged with patches of sentient oil (*The Pilot*, 2017).

Metebelis Spiders have been observed to teleport through time and space

TEMPORAL HAZARDS

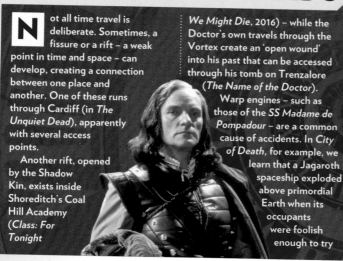

Not all time travel is deliberate. Sometimes, a fissure or a rift – a weak point in time and space – can develop, creating a connection between one place and another. One of these runs through Cardiff (in *The Unquiet Dead*), apparently with several access points.

Another rift, opened by the Shadow Kin, exists inside Shoreditch's Coal Hill Academy (*Class: For Tonight We Might Die*, 2016) – while the Doctor's own travels through the Vortex create an 'open wound' into his past that can be accessed through his tomb on Trenzalore (*The Name of the Doctor*).

Warp engines – such as those of the *SS Madame de Pompadour* – are a common cause of accidents. In *City of Death*, for example, we learn that a Jagaroth spaceship exploded above primordial Earth when its occupants were foolish enough to try to take off on warp drive. Scaroth, the only survivor, was flung into the Time Vortex and split into 12 different parts, which were scattered throughout the planet's history.

Another ship with warp drive, a 26th-century human freighter, jumped time warps when Cyber-technology interfered with its normal operations, hurling it some 65 million years back in time (*Earthshock*, 1982) – while a ship belonging to Mawdryn and his band of scientists was caught in a warp ellipse and thrown into a fixed orbit in time as well as space, though the cause of this is unclear (*Mawdryn Undead*, 1983).

(*Planet of the Spiders*, 1974), supposedly by psychic power alone – while a touch from a Weeping Angel can banish its victim to the past (*Blink*). Chronovores and Reapers live inside the Vortex, roaming where they will (in, respectively, *The Time Monster* and 2005's *Father's Day*) – while time-sensitive Tharils travel on the time winds (*Warriors' Gate*, 1981) that blow inside the Vortex (2013's *The Time of the Doctor*) – meaning that they too can traverse it unassisted, using natural gateways and – yes – mirrors as their access points.

Only one race, however, has refined time travel to the point where they can actually challenge the Time Lords.

The Daleks began, as have others, by creating time corridors (demonstrated in 1984's *Resurrection of the Daleks*, 2010's *Victory of the Daleks* and, with hindsight, *The Evil of the Daleks* too). They were typically ruthless, though, in their pursuit of greater power. At one point, they even acquired the Hand of Omega: the remote stellar manipulator that created the Time Lords' power source, the Eye of Harmony

(*Remembrance of the Daleks*, 1988). The Doctor thwarted them on this occasion, but already knew that they were destined to achieve their ambitions.

In both *The Chase* (1965) and *The Daleks' Master Plan* (1965-66), the Daleks pursue the Doctor's TARDIS in a time machine the equal of his own – if not a little bit faster and more accurate. In the latter story, they have also built a time-manipulating device that, betraying their all-too-predictable plans for it, they have christened the Time Destructor.

The Daleks once used time travel to rewrite their own history, reconquering Earth in the 22nd century (*Day of the Daleks*, 1972). During this period, they employed a portable time transmitter, which human rebels were able to steal, copy and use in an attempt to put things right. Later Dalek paradigms had equipment built into their casings, which allowed them to affect an emergency temporal shift when threatened (first seen in *Doomsday*, 2006).

After that, the ensuing Time War was perhaps inevitable... ⚛

Above left: Captain Tancredi (Julian Glover), aka Scaroth of the Jagaroth, in *City of Death*.

Top centre: The *SS Madame de Pompadour* in *The Girl in the Fireplace* (2006).

Top right: Mawydryn's ship in *Mawdryn Undead* (1983).

Above: A space freighter travels back 65 million years in *Earthshock* (1982).

Left: The giant spiders of Metebelis III in *Planet of the Spiders* (1974).

Below left: The Dalek time machine as seen in *The Chase* (1965).

Below right: The Daleks stored the deadly Movellan virus in the 20th century, at the other end of a time corridor – but Davros (Terry Molloy) used some of the virus to destroy his own creations in *Resurrection if the Daleks* (1984).

THE TARDIS

Much of the Doctor's incredible ship is shrouded in mystery, but we've discovered that it's far more than a machine for travelling through time and space...

FEATURE BY **JONATHAN MORRIS**

The TARDIS is, without doubt, the most extraordinary piece of technology in *Doctor Who*. The product of one of the most advanced civilisations in the universe, it's capable of many feats, not least its ability to travel anywhere through time and space. But how does it work?

To begin with, its primary power source is the Eye of Harmony, the source of energy that gives the Time Lords mastery over time. In *The Three Doctors* (1972-73) we learn that solar engineer Omega created this power source by detonating a star; in *The Deadly Assassin* (1976) its discovery is attributed to another Time Lord, Rassilon, and the power source is named as the Eye of Harmony, the stabilised nucleus of a black hole, relocated to an area beneath the Panopticon on Gallifrey. In *Hide* (2013) we learn that it's possible to create a 'subset' of the Eye, which may explain why the Eye is present in the TARDIS in the 1996 TV Movie and *Journey to the Centre of the TARDIS* (2013).

It's a little mind-boggling to fathom how the Eye can be present in every TARDIS, until you consider that the interior of every TARDIS exists in a different dimension (as explained in *The Robots of Death*, 1977). Presumably, just as the interior continua can intersect with real space-time through the door, it can also intersect with wherever the Eye is too; the Eye seen in the TARDIS is like the tip of an iceberg protruding into the TARDIS interior dimension while the rest of the Eye exists in real space-time. However, the power drains in *Death to the Daleks* (1974), *Enlightenment* (1983) and *Flatline* (2014) imply that the TARDIS' power supply is finite – so perhaps the TARDIS only intersects with the Eye when it needs to refuel? In *The Invasion of Time* (1978) we learn that the TARDIS has an *ancillary* power station (disguised as an art gallery); might this be how the TARDIS is powered when not relying on its *primary* power source?

THE TARDIS IS CAPABLE OF MANY FEATS, NOT LEAST ITS ABILITY TO TRAVEL THROUGH TIME AND SPACE.

Of course, after the Time War the Ninth Doctor believed Gallifrey to have been destroyed, which is why he refuels the TARDIS by landing on a rift in time and space, filling up the engines with rift energy. (See *Boom Town*, 2005; *Utopia*, 2007; *The Doctor's Wife*, 2011.) Dialogue in *The Doctor's Wife* implies that this is 'artron energy', although elsewhere this refers to the energy involved in Time Lord regeneration. *Rise of the Cybermen* (2006) seems to resolve this discrepancy when we learn ▶

THE TARDIS

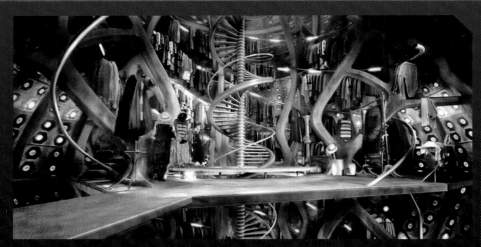

◄ that the TARDIS contains power cells that the Doctor can recharge using years of his life – ie, regeneration energy.

Whatever form the energy takes, in *Inside the Spaceship* (aka *The Edge of Destruction*, 1964) the Doctor claims the TARDIS power source (also "the heart of the machine") is located beneath the column of the console, with only the presence of the column preventing its escape. The motion of the column indicates the TARDIS being in flight, although debate surrounds the column's name. In spin-off media it's widely known as the Time Rotor, but on-screen it's only ever referred to as such in *The Doctor's Wife*. In *The Chase* (1965) and *Meglos* (1981) the term refers to an instrument on the console.

By *The Mind Robber* (1968) the TARDIS has a power room, then in *Journey to the Centre of the TARDIS* the Doctor and Clara visit the engine room (also referred to by the Doctor as "the heart of the TARDIS"); like the power station in *The Invasion of Time* its nature is concealed, this

TO ENSURE A SMOOTH LANDING YOU NEED TO SET THE SYNCHRONIC FEEDBACK CIRCUIT.

time by having its entrance disguised as a bottomless chasm.

In addition to the Eye and rift energy, there are other substances essential to the TARDIS' maintenance. Mercury provides the fluid link essential to transferring power for dematerialisation (see *The Mutants*, aka *The Daleks*, 1963-64; *The Web Planet*, 1965; *The Wheel in Space*, 1968; *Oxygen*, 2017), the mineral Zieton-7 serves to reline the trans-power system (*Vengeance on Varos*, 1985), and a Trachoid time crystal enables materialisation (*The Hand of Fear*, 1976).

So how exactly *does* the TARDIS materialise? First, you need to set the space-time co-ordinates in the directional unit (see *The Daleks' Master Plan*, 1965-66) or the landing circuit (*The Invasion*, 1968). If you want your destination to be a surprise, use the randomiser (*Destiny of the Daleks*, 1979) or let Harry Sullivan mess with the helmic regulator (*The Ark in Space*, 1975). As demonstrated by Romana in *The Pirate Planet* (1978), to ensure a smooth landing you need to set the synchronic feedback circuit and activate the multi-loop stabiliser. You shouldn't leave the brakes on, as they create a wheezing, groaning sound (*The Time of Angels*, 2010), and you should avoid jumping time tracks (*The Space Museum*, 1965). In an emergency, you can perform a random jump (*Frontier in Space*, 1973), a co-ordinate override (*Time-Flight*, 1982) or a materialisation flip-flop (*Warriors of the Deep*, 1984). If there's a critical timing

Above left: The TARDIS wardrobe in *The Christmas Invasion* (2005).

Above right: The Doctor and Clara (Jenna Coleman) take a leap of faith as they *Journey to the Centre of the TARDIS*.

Right: The Doctor tinkers with the remains of an abandoned TARDIS console in *The Doctor's Wife* (2011).

DESKTOP THEMES

The interior of the TARDIS is operated via 'architectural reconfiguration'. We see it in *Journey to the Centre of the TARDIS*, where it appears as a sort of phosphorescent root system. The same system is used to delete/jettison rooms in *Logopolis* and *Castrovalva*; the fact that it can reinvent the architecture explains why the TARDIS pool is present in *The Eleventh Hour* (2010) after being jettisoned shortly before *Paradise Towers* (1987). We also learn, in *The Doctor's Wife*, that the TARDIS can archive deleted rooms and that the Doctor can change the 'desktop' – for instance, the radical 'redecoration' of the control room seen in *The Time Monster* (1972). The Doctor closed the number two control room for "decoration" prior to *The Invisible Enemy* (1977); he hints that the TARDIS computer is responsible for the unimaginative colour scheme and starts manually repainting it in *Underworld* (1977).

Curiously, the extent of the TARDIS interior seems to have dramatically increased. *The Masque of Mandragora* (1976) introduces the idea of it having multiple control rooms along with various other rooms (including a swimming pool, a conservatory and a library, as well as innumerable corridors). Prior to that, the interior consisted of the control room and living quarters (plus a wardrobe), with Barbara only taking a couple of minutes to search the ship in *The Keys of Marinus* (1964). Quite how and why the TARDIS expanded is a mystery, but perhaps the redecoration in *The Time Monster* was the result of the Doctor familiarising himself with the architectural reconfiguration system?

malfunction, the TARDIS itself may instigate an automatic emergency landing (the TV Movie). The TARDIS will then materialise, although only its outer shell will exist as a real space-time event (*Logopolis*, 1981).

The TARDIS has several landing modes. It can hover (as in *Time-Flight*), land silently (many of its early landings were silent, but the Doctor first did so deliberately in *The Impossible Astronaut*, 2011) and invisibly – achieved unintentionally through a faulty visual stabiliser circuit in *The Invasion* (1968) before being performed purposely in *The Impossible Astronaut*. It can also land by descending from the skies – accidentally in *Fury from the Deep* (1968), deliberately in *The Name of the Doctor* (2013) – and fly, as in *The Runaway Bride* (2006).

Of course, the TARDIS' outer plasmic shell is supposed to be disguised, but it has been stuck in the form of a police box ever since *100,000 BC* (aka *An Unearthly Child*, 1963). The cloaking device (as it's described in the TV Movie) is the chameleon circuit; first named in *Logopolis*, it's also referred to as the camouflage unit in *The Time Meddler* (1965). The TARDIS was due to have the circuit repaired when the Doctor

stole it (*The Name of the Doctor*); the Doctor's efforts to repair it in *Logopolis* and *Attack of the Cybermen* (1985) both ended in failure, while in *Journey's End* (2008) Doctor-Donna realised that it could be repaired by "hot-binding the fragment links and superseding the binary..." before losing her thread.

The fact that the TARDIS' chameleon circuit was malfunctioning should, perhaps, have been obvious to the Doctor even before its landing on prehistoric Earth. As Ian Chesterton observed, police boxes are usually on the street, not in junkyards, and perhaps the sign saying 'Pull to Open' when it opens inwards should have been another clue. The circuit's unreliability could also account for the inconsistencies in the TARDIS' police box disguise, as noted by the First Doctor in *Twice Upon a Time* (2017) – "It seems to have expanded!"

The Twelfth Doctor attributes the increase in size to "all those years of [being] bigger on the inside". Whether or not he meant this seriously, it does tie in with the giant TARDIS seen in *The Name of the Doctor*, caused by the 'dimension dams' breaking down. As mentioned earlier, the TARDIS interior exists in another dimension. Indeed, according to Susan in *100,000 BC*, that's what Time And Relative Dimension In Space *means* – that the interior is a 'relative dimension' nested within the dimension of space. This ▶

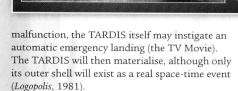

Above left: The secondary control room, first seen in *The Masque of Mandragora* (1976).

Above right: The Doctor and Romana look at the TARDIS scanner in *Full Circle*.

Left: The 'yearometer' in the TV Movie.

Below left: Idris (Suranne Jones) becomes the TARDIS itself in *The Doctor's Wife*.

Below right: Peri (Nicola Bryant) and the Doctor (Colin Baker) use seatbelts in *Timelash* (1985).

◀ would account for the occasions when the interior has tilted or shaken as a result of the exterior being tilted or shaken. (*Time-Flight* actually addresses this point, as the Doctor is able to change the interior orientation at the flick of a switch.) We know from *The Time Meddler* and *The War Games* (1969) that the system responsible for maintaining the interior is the 'dimension control' and that the removal of the 'time vector generator' will transform the interior into that of an everyday telephone box (*The Wheel in Space*); in *Father's Day* (2005), what the Doctor describes as a "wound in time" causes a similar effect.

Once the TARDIS has landed, it needs to check its surroundings are safe, using the radiation counter (introduced in *100,000 BC*), and assess the air and temperature (a procedure introduced in *The Rescue*, 1965). It can also detect motion (*The Aztecs*, 1964), gravity (*The Chase*), rain (*The Stones of Blood*, 1978), seismic activity (*Destiny of the Daleks*, 1979), energy fields (*The Awakening*, 1984) and time distortion (*The Mark of the Rani*, 1985). The 'yearometer' is another part of its central console that was first seen in *100,000 BC*.

More usefully, there's the scanner, which can give a panoramic view and also sound, when the audio link-up is working (*Arc of Infinity*, 1983). *Enlightenment* implies that the scanner camera is located in the police box light; however, in *The Three Doctors* it shows the TARDIS itself, suggesting that the 'image translator' can show a view from nearby co-ordinates (*Full Circle*, 1981). This could also explain how the Time Lords used the TARDIS to record scenes in what the Valeyard calls its "collection range" (*The Trial of a Time Lord*, 1986). The scanner was also used as a 'time scanner' in *The Moonbase* (1967) in order to glimpse into the future. According to the Doctor, however, "it's not very reliable" – which might explain why it was never used again.

Despite being indestructible (according to the Doctor in *The Curse of Peladon*, 1972), the TARDIS has numerous safety and defence systems. Some of these work effectively – for example, TARDIS will indicate a 'boundary error' if it travels too far into the future (*Frontios*, 1984) – while others are less helpful. In *The Wheel in Space*, for instance, the TARDIS is only able to report a fault through cryptic images on the scanner. This, however, is more useful than the TARDIS suffering 'indigestion' in its reluctance to land in *The Impossible Planet* (2006) and *Under the Lake* (2015), or flying to the end of the universe in an attempt to rid itself of Jack Harkness in *Utopia* (2007).

The TARDIS seatbelts (*Timelash*, 1985), emergency oxygen supply (*Planet of the Daleks*, 1973) and gas masks (*Rise of the Cybermen*) all prove useless, while the state of 'temporal grace'

BACK-SEAT DRIVER

It was originally part of the format of *Doctor Who* that the Doctor couldn't control the TARDIS. Indeed, he needs to appropriate the 'directional unit' from the Monk's TARDIS in order to return to Kembel in *The Daleks' Master Plan*. The Doctor's companions suspect that the fault lies elsewhere. ("The Doctor isn't very reliable," says Ian in the 1964 story *Marco Polo*.) The Doctor, however, asserts that the problem is merely a "technical hitch" (*The Time Meddler*, 1965) and that the "directional mechanism" is at fault (*The War Games*, 1969). Even so, he manages a fairly accurate landing in *The Web of Fear* (1968) – "half a mile on from where we expected to land" – and in *The Savages* (1966) the Elders anticipate the TARDIS' arrival as if its travels aren't completely unpredictable.

The Master describes the Doctor's TARDIS as a "museum piece" in *The Claws of Axos* (1972), although soon after this the intercession of the Time Lords in *Colony in Space* (1972) and the installation of a new dematerialisation circuit in *The Three Doctors* mean that the TARDIS' navigational systems are in full working order. Subsequent unintentional landings can only be the result of pilot error. Or can they? Because in *The Doctor's Wife* we learn that the TARDIS itself was responsible for all those 'mistaken' landings – "I always took you where you needed to go."

(mentioned in *The Hand of Fear*, 1976) fails to work so often that it's no surprise it turns out to have been a clever lie (*Let's Kill Hitler*, 2011). The TARDIS fault locator fails to give the location of a fault in *Inside the Spaceship* and fails to detect that TARDIS has miniaturised in *Planet of Giants* (1964). The Hostile Action Displacement System, introduced in *The Krotons* (1968-69), has – when switched on – the unfortunate effect of leaving the Doctor and his companion in peril (*Cold War*, 2013), and the TARDIS' 'siege mode', activated in *Flatline*, has the inconvenient flaw that it can't be switched off during a power outage.

There's also the Cloister Bell, introduced in *Logopolis* as a communications device reserved for wild catastrophes but established in *Castrovalva* (1982) as an unhelpfully non-specific warning of imminent disaster. By the time of *Let's Kill Hitler* and *Hide* (2013), the TARDIS has a more user-friendly voice/visual interface, while the most useful safety system must be Emergency Program One, which takes Rose home in *The*

DESPITE BEING INDESTRUCTIBLE, THE TARDIS HAS NUMEROUS SAFETY AND DEFENCE SYSTEMS.

Parting of the Ways (2005) – and which presumably takes Clara home, too, in *The Time of the Doctor* (2013). The TARDIS' other communication devices include interior and exterior telephones and the telepathic circuit. This is responsible for generating the telepathic field which translates alien languages (although 2005's *The Christmas Invasion* establishes that it requires a conscious Time Lord as intermediary). The circuit can also be used for navigation (*The Name of the Doctor*) and to send messages (*Frontier in Space*).

The TARDIS' exterior is protected by a defensive mechanism; it repels a Zarbi that attempts to enter in *The Web Planet* and (mostly) keeps out water in *The War Games* before being

established as a force field in *The Three Doctors*. Also referred to as a defence shield, it can be extended to create a tunnel of air, first seen in *The Horns of Nimon* (1979-80) and later used in *The Time of Angels* and *Oxygen*. The force field/ defence shield also protects the TARDIS when in the Vortex; it's lowered in *The Doctor's Wife* and extended to protect Clara in *The Time of the Doctor*. In addition, the TARDIS can generate a gravity tractor beam strong enough to divert a neutron star (*The Creature from the Pit*, 1979), pull a rocket from a black hole (*The Satan Pit*, 2006) and even move the Earth (*Journey's End*).

In summary, there's almost nothing the TARDIS can't do – except it has no offensive capabilities of any kind and its navigational and defence systems are hopelessly unreliable. But, across 55 years of *Doctor Who*, we've barely scratched the surface; there is also the food machine, the astral map, the information system and the chameleon arch, amongst others. Its systems are as infinite as its rooms, all just waiting to be explored. It is, literally and figuratively, bigger on the inside. 🜨

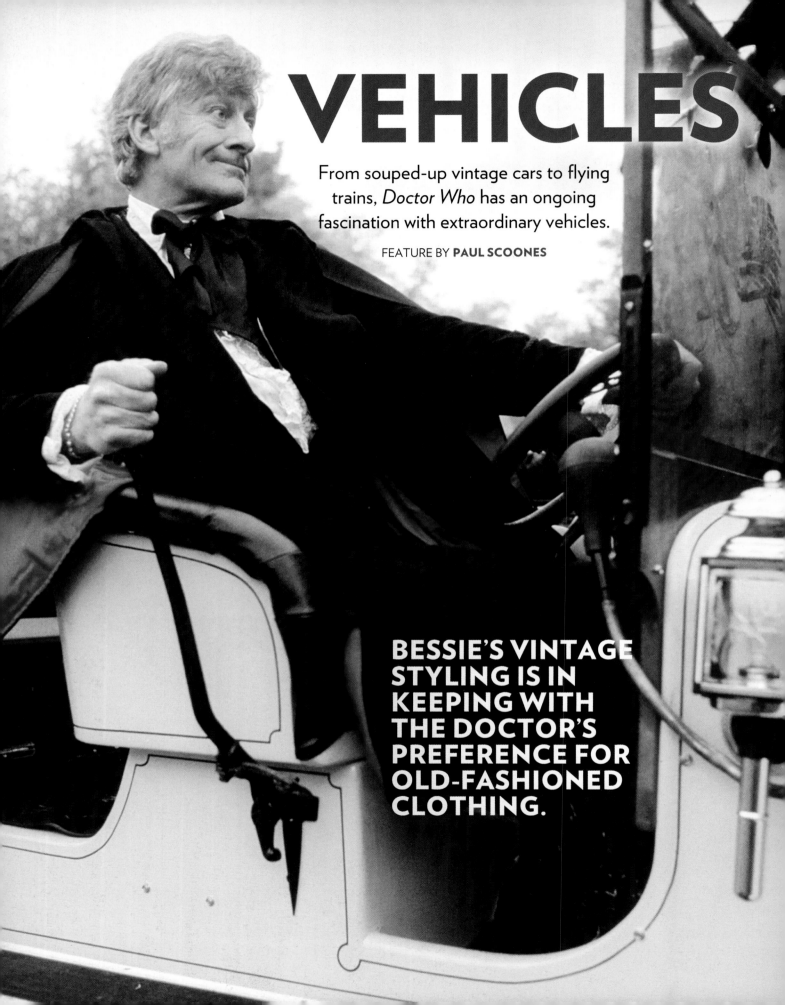

VEHICLES

From souped-up vintage cars to flying trains, *Doctor Who* has an ongoing fascination with extraordinary vehicles.

FEATURE BY **PAUL SCOONES**

BESSIE'S VINTAGE STYLING IS IN KEEPING WITH THE DOCTOR'S PREFERENCE FOR OLD-FASHIONED CLOTHING.

When the newly regenerated Third Doctor is sent to Earth by the Time Lords, the conditions of his exile dictate that the TARDIS is out of action due to a disabled dematerialisation circuit – also, that he is prevented from accessing his memories of time travel theory. Without the means or the knowledge to travel in space and time, the Doctor is forced to rely on more conventional means of travel. While chafing at the limitations imposed on him, the Doctor gains a new appreciation for both driving, and working on, Earth vehicles.

The Doctor's love affair with the motor car begins in *Spearhead from Space* (1970), when he steals a 1927 Vauxhall 14/40 Princeton tourer from Ashbridge Cottage Hospital in order to travel to UNIT HQ in London. At the story's conclusion, he tells Brigadier Lethbridge-Stewart, "I took to that car. It had character." Although he reluctantly concedes that it has to be returned to its rightful owner, the Doctor asks the Brigadier to find him "something similar".

That similar something turns out to be Bessie, a yellow, vintage-style, open-topped car introduced in the opening episode of *Doctor Who and the Silurians* (1970). The Doctor affectionately addresses the car by name and refers to it using feminine pronouns. It's unclear if the Doctor dubbed the car Bessie or if it already had the name when he acquired it. He informs a sceptical Liz Shaw that his car is "of great character" and that he was "very lucky to get her".

Bessie's vintage styling is in keeping with the Doctor's preference for old-fashioned clothing. Like the Time Lord, the car's outward appearance belies its true nature. Bessie is no ordinary vintage motor car; thanks to the Doctor's improvements it's enhanced with numerous advanced technological gadgets.

When Bessie is first seen, the Doctor has only recently acquired her, and he finishes work on modifications in preparation for taking the car out for a trial run. The first hint of the Doctor's unconventional alterations to his car comes at the end of the story. When Bessie breaks down, the Doctor coaxes the car back into life by pouring a small vial of liquid into the radiator and waiting a few moments for the substance to work its way through the car and dribble out of the exhaust pipe. This prompts the engine to start.

In *The Ambassadors of Death* (1970), the car is revealed to be fitted with an 'Anti Thief Device' (according to the labelled switch on Bessie's dashboard). When activated, this generates a force field causing anyone touching the car to become stuck to it. The effect wears off after a short time, leading the Doctor to conclude that the field strength needs to be increased.

The Doctor fits Bessie with a radio-control unit so that he can operate the car remotely. This comes in useful in *The Dæmons* (1971), when he demonstrates to the villagers at Devil's End the difference between science and magic, and later in preventing the Master from evading capture by stealing Bessie.

In *The Mutants* (1972), the Doctor is seen in his laboratory working on a 'minimum inertia superdrive' for Bessie. By the ▶

Opposite page: A publicity shot of Jon Pertwee (as the Doctor) in Bessie from *Doctor Who and the Silurians* (1970).

Above: Pertwee, Caroline John (as Liz Shaw) and Bessie, in a publicity shot taken at the Thames Embankment on 13 January 1970.

Inset left: The Doctor steals a car in Episode 2 of *Spearhead from Space* (1970).

Bottom left: The dashboard Anti Thief Device switch, as seen in *The Ambassadors of Death* (1970).

Left A rear view of Bessie, pictured at the *Doctor Who Experience* in 2013.
Photo © Marcus Hearn

ANTI THIEF DEVICE

WHO 1

VEHICLES

Above left: Sylvester McCoy (as the Doctor), Sophie Aldred (as Ace) and Bessie on location for the recording of *Battlefield* in May 1989.

Above right: The 'Whomobile' in *Planet of the Spiders* (1974).

Right inset: The Doctor makes a 'minimum inertia overdrive' for Bessie in Episode One of *The Mutants* (1972).

Below left: The cover of Peter Filby's 1977 reference book.

Below right: Bessie's distinctive number plate. Photo © Marcus Hearn.

◄ next story, *The Time Monster* (1972), Bessie has been fitted with the device, which gives the car the ability to travel at exceptionally high speeds. When Bessie comes to a sudden stop, its occupants are protected by the car's brakes, which work by absorbing inertia – including that of the passengers. The Doctor alludes to his many modifications to the vehicle, telling Jo Grant that "Bessie's no ordinary car".

When Bessie returns after a long absence in *Battlefield* (1989), the Seventh Doctor attaches a control device to the steering wheel hub that allows the car to travel at speed, leaving behind a set of flaming tyre marks. This previously unseen device may have been an updated version of the superdrive.

Bessie wasn't the Third Doctor's only road vehicle – he also drove a sleek, futuristic-looking two-seater that was first seen in *Invasion of the Dinosaurs* (1974). This silver car glides across

the ground like a hovercraft, the Doctor utilising it to drive around London's evacuated streets. The cockpit dashboard is fitted with advanced-looking features that include a television screen and a 'computer bank'. In the camera script for *Invasion of the Dinosaurs* Part Four, a couple of trims to the dialogue lost the reveal that the Doctor had built the car, and the Brigadier describing it as "that flying saucer effort".

This car was never given a name on screen, but in reality it was named 'Alien' by its manufacturer. In scripts, as well as in reference books and articles, it's referred to as the 'Whomobile'. For the purposes of the Driver and Vehicle Licensing Agency it was registered as a combination of both titles: 'Whomobile Alien'. This custom vehicle may have had two names, but it was a one-off commissioned and paid for

BUILDING BESSIE

Bessie was constructed from a fibreglass kit known as 'The Edwardian' which was marketed to car-building hobbyists. The kits were produced as a joint venture between Siva Engineering in Bournemouth and Neville Trickett (Design) Ltd in Blandford, Dorset. The Edwardian kit was designed to fit over the engine and chassis of the E93A Ford Popular. It was also possible to purchase a complete car from Siva Sales in Weymouth, Dorset.

According to Peter Filby, author of the 1977 book *British Specialist Cars Volume 2: Roadsters/Replicas and Fun Cars*, the Edwardian was initially produced as a two-seater roadster model, but a four-seater

tourer version was added shortly afterwards. The first Siva Edwardian car was completed just in time to go on display at the West Hants Show in Bournemouth in May 1969. The Edwardian kits were available for

five years, during which time Filby estimates that around 80 tourer and 25 roadster body kits were constructed in total.

Former *Doctor Who* assistant script editor Trevor Ray recalls that he saw an item on a television programme about the makers of the car kits. This led to the production

office making arrangements to purchase an assembled Edwardian tourer in time for the filming of *Doctor Who and the Silurians* in November 1969. As the copyright in Bessie's design was owned by Siva, the BBC had to pay the company a fee whenever Bessie was featured on *Doctor Who* merchandise.

by Jon Pertwee. Producer Barry Letts allowed its use in the series, but this was towards the end of Pertwee's tenure and the Whomobile ultimately only featured in two episodes. The new car made its second and final appearance in *Planet of the Spiders* (1974), in which it's revealed, to the surprise of Sarah Jane Smith, that the car has the ability to fly. The Brigadier hinted at this in *Invasion of the Dinosaurs* when he said, "You'll never get it off the ground" – but in this episode he seems just as unaware of the car's powers of flight. Incidentally, Bessie and the Doctor's new car seem fairly evenly matched for speed on the ground. In a chase along country lanes, Bessie, driven by the Brigadier, manages to keep up with the Doctor's new car, driven by Lupton. A policeman joins the chase and observes that both vehicles travel at speeds up to 90 miles an hour. Initially fitted with a temporary windscreen for its first appearance in *Invasion of the Dinosaurs*, the new car had acquired a custom-made canopy for its second outing.

T he Doctor has never seemed inclined to acquire or build another vehicle. There are, however, numerous other examples of technologically advanced modes of transport.

The Time Lady Romana seems to share the Doctor's interest in vehicles. She remembers being given an air car for her 70th birthday, implying that these craft were in use on her home planet Gallifrey. Air cars, small flying vehicles

with limited passenger capacity, are also used on Zanak (*The Pirate Planet*, 1978), where they're the favoured means of transportation around the planet for the Captain's guards. The Zanak air car resembles a speedboat. Romana suggests that the Zanak aircars' speed and energy efficiency could be significantly improved by realigning the magnetic vectors and fitting a polarity oscillator. ▶

Left: The air car featured in *The Pirate Planet* (1978).

Above: The Doctor (Tom Baker) and Kimus (David Warwick) take to the skies in *The Pirate Planet*.

Below: Jon Pertwee took pride in the fact that, despite its unusual design, the Whomobile was legal to drive on British roads.

THE 'WHOMOBILE' WAS A ONE-OFF COMMISSION AND PAID FOR BY JON PERTWEE.

VEHICLES

Above left: Stacked vehicles in *Gridlock* (2007).

Above right: The Androzani Harvester in *The Doctor, the Widow and the Wardrobe* (2011).

Right inset: The sandminer in *The Robots of Death* (1977).

Below: Brannigan (Ardal O'Hanlan) and Valerie (Jennifer Hennessey) behind the wheel, in a publicity shot from *Gridlock*.

◄ A multitude of small box-shaped hovering cars are home to most of the surviving population of New New York on New Earth in *Gridlock* (2007). The cars are lined up in rows on the enclosed, smog-filled Undercity Motorway, moving along the heavily congested route at a rate of just five miles every 12 years. Some of the occupants have been living in their cars for up to 23 years. The cars are self-contained living habitats that recycle waste products as food, and an onboard computer keeps the occupants in regular contact with each other. The cars are outwardly identical in size and shape, but the interiors have been customised by their occupants as miniature homes.

An Androzani Harvester, a massive, yellow, three-legged walker, patrols a forest of Androzani trees in *The Doctor, the Widow and the Wardrobe* (2011). The walker is topped by a control platform and cockpit, crewed by three military personnel – Droxil, Billis and Ven-Garr – from Androzani Major in the year 5345. The piston-powered legs are large enough to house an elevator carrying several humans. The Harvester's role is apparently to scan the forest in preparation for harvesting the trees, which are melted down with acid rain to create battery fluid.

Another vehicle used to reap a planet's natural resources is the sandminer in *The Robots of Death* (1977). Storm Mine 4, with its crew of humans and robots, traces and extracts valuable ore from sands in a vast uncharted desert on an alien planet. The miner is steered into sand storms where it extracts the heavier elements using scoops and gathers the ore in hoppers. Storm Mine 4's mission is planned to last two years and the vehicle is fitted with luxurious living quarters for the comfort of its human crew. Motive units keep the miner from sinking into the sands. The miner has a life-support plant as well as refrigeration and filtering systems, and the water is recycled.

THE CARS ARE LINED UP IN ROWS ON THE ENCLOSED, SMOG-FILLED UNDERCITY MOTORWAY.

CAR TROUBLE

Bessie is often described as an 'Edwardian roadster' but this is a misnomer. The car isn't from the Edwardian era, and neither is she a roadster.

The phrase makes an early appearance in the *Radio Times* cover-dated 29 January 1970, where writer Roger Baker observes that Bessie 'looks like an Edwardian roadster'. *The Making of Doctor Who* by Malcolm Hulke and Terrance Dicks (1972) calls the car 'a colourful very old-fashioned roadster'. The following year *Radio Times* offered up 'sprightly yellow roadster' in its 1973 *Doctor Who* special, a phrase later used in the revised edition of *The Making*

of *Doctor Who* (1976) and Jean-Marc Lofficier's *The Doctor Who Programme Guide* (1981). Terrance Dicks often describes Bessie as an 'Edwardian roadster' in his Target novelisations; in publication order the term first appears in *Doctor Who and the Giant Robot* (1975).

In motoring terminology, a 'roadster' is typically defined as an open-top two-seat car, whereas a 'tourer' is an open-top car seating four or more. 'Edwardian roadster' is almost certainly derived from the name given to the custom car kit used to construct Bessie. The manufacturers named it 'The Edwardian' as it was inspired by vintage

cars of the early 1900s. Kits were available in both two-seater and four-seater versions, and as Bessie is the latter, it's more accurate to describe the car as a tourer.

In *Midnight* (2008), the Crusader 50 bus operated by the Leisure Planet Company takes tourists on a journey across the surface of the diamond planet Midnight. The planet's airless and heavily radioactive environment is hostile to life. The Crusader Tours bus, described by the Tenth Doctor as "a big space truck", is heavily shielded, with windows made of 'Finitoglass'. The bus is powered by a 'micropetrol' engine and has a life-support system that can provide air for ten years. The Crusader 50 has a crew of three: a driver, a mechanic and a hostess. A passenger entertainment system provides channels showing 'Earth classics', including music videos and cartoons. The Crusader 50 tour departs from the Leisure Palace and travels 500 kilometres in four hours to reach the Multifaceted Coast, the Sapphire Waterfall and the Cliffs of Oblivion.

The *Orient Express* also takes its passengers on an unusual sightseeing trip, in *Mummy on the Orient Express* (2014). As the Twelfth Doctor explains, the train is a "completely faithful recreation of the original *Orient Express*, except slightly bigger, and in space". The train travels on hyperspace ribbons rather than rails. It's operated by United Galaxy Tours and controlled by a sentient computer system known as Gus. Some of the train's passengers and interior decor are hard-light holograms, and the train is fitted out with a technologically advanced laboratory.

In similar vein, the *Titanic*, a recreation of the famous doomed passenger liner that sank on its maiden voyage in 1912, operates as an advanced spacefaring vessel. The spaceship is a Max Capricorn cruise liner, travelling from the planet Sto to Earth, in *Voyage of the Damned* (2007). The ship is powered by a nuclear storm drive and its robotic crew

are referred to as the Heavenly Host. Teleportation devices transport passengers and crew to and from the vessel.

The *Valiant* is a huge aircraft carrier hovering in Earth's atmosphere, first seen in *The Sound of Drums/Last of the Time Lords* (2007). It's commanded by UNIT and described by Captain Jack Harkness as "a ship for the 21st century, protecting the skies of planet Earth." The Master, in his guise as Harold Saxon, helped design the ship while working for the Ministry of Defence. Following the Master's defeat, UNIT continued to use the *Valiant* for home world security, utilising its massive jet turbine engines to dispel toxic gas into the atmosphere in *The Poison Sky* (2008). The ship is attacked by the Daleks in *The Stolen Earth* (2008) but apparently survives the engagement, as the *Valiant* continues to be used by UNIT, according to Kate Lethbridge-Stewart in *Death in Heaven* (2014). The Twelfth Doctor jokingly calls it Cloudbase, a reference to its similarity to the airborne headquarters of the Spectrum Organisation in the Gerry Anderson television series *Captain Scarlet and the Mysterons* (1967-68).

A floating aircraft carrier shouldn't have come as a surprise to viewers – ever since a police box was revealed to be machine for travelling through time and space, *Doctor Who* has frequently subverted our expectations of the seemingly mundane vehicles it has depicted.

Above: Elisabeth Sladen (as Sarah Jane Smith), Tom Baker (as the Doctor) and Bessie, pictured during the recording of *Robot* on 2 May 1974.

Left inset: The train in space in *Mummy on the Orient Express* (2014).

Below inset: The *Titanic* approaches Earth in *Voyage of the Damned* (2007).

Bottom left: The *Valiant* in *The Sound of Drums* (2007).

Bottom right: Sky (Lesley Sharpe) aboard the ill-fated Crusader 50 bus in *Midnight* (2008).

VIRTUAL REALITIES

The universe can be a strange and challenging place. But the environments found within virtual worlds can be even more terrifying...

FEATURE BY **MARK WRIGHT**

Opposite page: Amy (Karen Gillan) and Rory (Arthur Darvill) are trapped in a virtual hotel in *The God Complex* (2011).

Below: William Gibson's *Neuromancer* was first published in 1984.

Bottom left: Jamie (Hamish Wilson), the Doctor (Patrick Troughton) and Zoe (Wendy Padbury) meet Lemuel Gulliver (Bernard Horsfall) and clockwork robots in *The Mind Robber* (1968).

Bottom right: The Doctor (Matt Smith) has to face his worst fear in *The God Complex*.

Virtual realities or worlds encompass a wide range of manifestations. From the advanced science of the Time Lords' Matrix to the vast, life-saving CAL computer of the Library, or an alien device worn on the wrist, the virtual worlds experienced by the Doctor across the universe don't conform to a single categorisation.

In purely technological terms, a virtual world can be anything constituting an artificially generated, three-dimensional environment that a being can explore and interact with, manipulating objects and communicating with personalities generated by that system.

Science fiction has had a long flirtation with virtual worlds, one of the first instances being Stanley G Weinbaum's 1935 short story *Pygmalion's Spectacles*, with its visionary depiction of a system comprising a pair of goggles that allow the wearer to experience another world through holograms and stimulating the senses. Weinbaum's vision wasn't a million light years away from the consumable virtual reality technology available today.

Novelist William Gibson introduced the term 'cyberspace' in his 1982 short story *Burning Chrome*, expanding on this concept of vast, networked virtual spaces – or matrixes – in the novel *Neuromancer* (1984). Gibson's concepts were pushed further on screen by the Wachowski Brothers' 1999 film *The Matrix*, which remains one of cinema's most celebrated depictions of a virtual world. It riffs on themes of philosophy and that uncanny feeling that the world we inhabit isn't quite what it seems to be. Prior to that, Disney's *Tron* (1982) depicted a computer world populated with humanoid embodiments of programs slaved to the Master Control Program, entered by human programmer Flynn.

SCIENCE FICTION HAS HAD A LONG FLIRTATION WITH VIRTUAL WORLDS.

In terms of plot generation, the most fertile virtual world depicted on screen was the *Star Trek* franchise's 'holodeck', which debuted in the pilot episode of *Star Trek: The Next Generation* (1987). This immersive holographic system was a recreational area aboard the *USS Enterprise* that could easily supply a whole season's worth of plots – and then some. Episodes on this theme depicted the seductive lure of immersing oneself in a virtual world when the real world becomes too difficult, questioning the sentience of the virtual beings generated on the holodeck.

Over the decades, the *Doctor Who* universe has thrown up a wide variety of different takes on virtual worlds. Some represent fully technological virtual realities, others are a mesh of technology, organic life and imagination, while there are also those that are simply a quirk of natural phenomena, where science and magic are indistinguishable.

Chronologically speaking, the Doctor's earliest ingress into a virtual world is a disorientating trip into the Land of Fiction in *The Mind Robber* (1968). Following an emergency ▶

Above left: Clockwork soldiers stand to attention in *The Mind Robber*.

Above right: A young girl teaches the Doctor (Peter Davison) how to count in the imaginary domain of *Castrovalva* (1982).

Below left: Zoe is enticed to enter a virtual world in *The Mind Robber*.

Below centre: The Karkus (Christopher Robbie), a comic-book character brought to life in *The Mind Robber*.

Below right: The baffling topography of Castrovalva.

relocation, the Doctor, Jamie and Zoe find themselves in a world populated by fictional characters, including Rapunzel, Lemuel Gulliver of *Gulliver's Travels* and the Karkus, a comic-book character from the *Space Time Telegraph* loved by Zoe.

At the heart of this world, the Doctor discovers the Master of the Land of Fiction, a tragic human writer who has been enslaved by the Master Brain, a computer of unknown origin that uses the power of his imagination to create this virtual world and the characters populating it. There are elements of the Land of Fiction that mark it out as a natural phenomenon, a pocket universe perhaps, but the Doctor's interactions with the environment and fictional characters can be interpreted as a virtual reality combining the power of organic thought to maintain a world through advanced, alien technology.

VIRTUAL REALITY CAN BE PUT TO NUMEROUS USES – ENTERTAINMENT, RESEARCH, EVEN IMPRISONMENT.

The Land of Fiction shares some commonality with another virtual world that may help explain the true nature of that realm. After failing to murder the newly regenerated Doctor, Tegan and Nyssa by plunging the TARDIS into the hydrogen inrush of Event One, the Master has an insidious back-up scheme, "a trap behind that trap that would have been a joy to spring" (*Castrovalva*, 1982). Standing atop a mountain on a verdant alien world, the picturesque and simple town of Castrovalva is the perfect place for the Doctor to recuperate, but it's never really there. The dwellings, walkways, squares and even the people that populate Castrovalva are brought into being by Logopolitan block transfer computation and the mathematical brilliance of the captive Adric. With Adric trapped in a web of deadly hadron power lines, it's this technology that maintains the world that the Doctor, Nyssa and Tegan are able to interact with.

It's uncertain whether the population of Castrovalva are sentient in any way, which throws up complex questions about the nature of virtually manifested life. Librarian

Shardovan certainly has an inkling as to the artificial nature of his existence, which gives the Doctor a vital clue to escaping the Master's scheme before Castrovalva implodes in on itself, leaving the Master imprisoned in his own virtual creation.

As the technology advanced to become more accessible, not every virtual world had to be a fully immersive environment with detailed simulacra; they could merely be a tool to achieve a wider purpose. In *City of Death* (1979), Count Scarlioni – aka Scaroth, last of the Jagaroth – proposes to fund experiments in time travel by stealing the *Mona Lisa* and selling multiple copies on the black market. To plan the theft, Countess Scarlioni records an image of the Louvre from a bracelet. "A useful little device: wear it always," Scarlioni tells her. The bracelet projects an immersive rendering of the gallery space that Scarlioni's men can fully interact with in planning the heist down to the last detail. It's the advanced nature of the device on the Countess' wrist that alerts the Doctor to the intrigue during his Paris holiday with Romana.

Shortly after their Paris sojourn, the Doctor and Romana become involved with an intergalactic accident that fuses the spacecraft *Hecate* with the cruise-liner *Empress* in a hyperspace collision (*Nightmare of Eden*, 1979). One of the curious elements of this adventure is their meeting with xenozoologist Tryst, inventor of the Continuous Event Transmuter (CET). In essence a sophisticated slide show to store a matter transmutation of the environments and lifeforms Tryst has visited, the CET "allows us to see them whenever we wish. The flora and the fauna are actually in a crystal." Romana is instantly alerted to the

DREAM STATES

Not every virtual world is created through technology. There are some that would be perceived by certain cultures as the result of magic and mysticism, and others that are quirks of the natural world.

On Deva Loka, the world of the Kinda tribe, Tegan finds herself entering a nightmare dream world generated by a collection of wind chimes (*Kinda*, 1982). This world has a physicality and Tegan is able to interact with the beings she finds there, although it's unclear if she's really there or if it's all in her mind. Through this world and Tegan, the Mara establishes a foothold in the physical universe. While this has elements of what could be termed magic, the wind chimes – and other Kinda artefacts such as the Box of Jhana – could be considered a higher form of technology.

The Doctor, Amy and Rory experience environments that are indistinguishable from reality when the TARDIS comes under the influence of a being called the Dream Lord (*Amy's Choice*, 2010). Amy is given a choice to determine which environment is the real world and which is a 'dream' – the TARDIS control room, or the village of Leadworth. Each world feels physical and real; however, both worlds and the Dream Lord are generated by a rogue particle of 'psychic pollen'. It's also possible that the Dream Lord is a manifestation of the Doctor's inner personality.

Other distinctive virtual worlds are created through more recognisable means. In *The Name of the Doctor* (2013), Victorian detective Madame Vastra is able to summon her associates to a 'conference call' across time and space through a narcotic delivered by means of a burning candle, or a piece of paper laced with the soporific. On handling a letter sent from Vastra, Clara finds herself sitting in a Chinese-themed room alongside Vastra, Jenny Flint, Strax and River Song, with River's presence pulled from another virtual world – that of the Library's CAL hard drive. Within this dream reality, the guests can interact with each other. Vastra even uses her memories to create a favourite tea, which she pours for her guests.

dangerous failings of Tryst's "crude form of matter transfer by dimensional control". The localised effects of the hyperspace collision cause dangerous instabilities, allowing anybody to literally step inside the landscape images projected by the CET's crystals – and for savage Mandrel, native to the planet Eden, to step out and rampage through the corridors of the *Empress*.

Virtual reality technology can be put to numerous uses – entertainment, scientific research, subjugation of humanity, even imprisonment. *The God Complex* (2011) ▶

Above left: Using the virtual reality bracelet in *City of Death* (1979).

Above centre: Madame Vastra (Neve McIntosh) hosts a virtual tea party in *The Name of the Doctor* (2013).

Above right: Tegan (Janet Fielding) is trapped in a dream world in *Kinda* (1982).

Below left: The Doctor gets a geography lesson from Mergrave (Michael Sheard) in *Castrovalva*.

Below right: Mandrels break out from the CET machine in *Nightmare of Eden* (1979).

Above left: As the Minotaur dies, reality is revealed in *The God Complex*.

Above right: The Doctor and Webley (Jason Watkins) are augmented with Cyber technology in *Nightmare in Silver* (2013).

Far right: Donna (Catherine Tate) is uploaded to the computer in *Silence in the Library* (2008)

Below: Time Vortex, a 'virtual reality' *Doctor Who* game released in 2017.

Bottom left: The 1958 edition of this anthology contained the first published use of the term 'virtual reality'.

Bottom right: River Song and her dead crew survive in the virtual world of the Library.

◄ sees the Doctor, Amy Pond and Rory Williams landing in what they think is a hotel, but the Doctor knows better. "Who would mock up an Earth hotel?" wonders Rory; the answer is at once terrifying and tragic. Forced together with a group of mismatched humans and aliens, the time travellers are stalked through the maze-like hotel corridors by an ancient Minotaur creature that feeds off faith, with the rooms corresponding to the deepest fears of the group members. The Doctor realises that they're aboard a prison ship built for the ancient creature, with the hotel a sophisticated virtual projection that shifts around their movements. Released from its captivity, the creature dies in the Doctor's arms and the hotel corridors shimmer away to be replaced by the empty prison ship and the systems that generated the virtual environment.

There are occasions when a virtual world – or what can be perceived as a fully immersive augmented reality – is projected within ourselves. Under the influence of Cybermites while on Hedgewick's World of Wonders, the Doctor's mind is subjugated into the Cyberiad, the Doctor becoming a new Cyber-Planner to lead the next generation of Cybermen (*Nightmare in Silver*, 2013). The ensuing mental battle between the Doctor and 'Mr Clever' for control of the Doctor's mind is represented as a physical, immersive reality, influenced by the meshing of Time Lord flesh with invading Cyber-technology.

The potential for virtual world-generating technology to be abused and perverted for evil is vast, but there are occasions when the technology is used altruistically, even if the results are hazardous. When flesh-eating Vashta Nerada hatched out on the planet-sized Library, the CAL artificial intelligence attempted to teleport over 4,000 people to safety (*Silence in the Library/Forest of the Dead*, 2008). Instead, the minds and bodies of the visitors were uploaded to CAL's hard drive, where they're kept in a dream state. When Donna Noble is uploaded to the hard drive, the 'data-ghost' of Miss Evangelista explains that "What you see around you, this entire world, is nothing more than a virtual reality." Before being rescued by the Doctor, Donna experiences a full virtual life involving marriage and children.

VIRTUAL ORIGINS

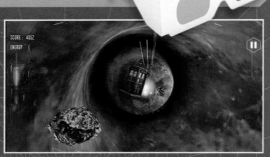

The origins of the concepts behind virtual reality are difficult to divine, but one of the first instances can be traced to the French dramatist Antonin Artaud (1896-1948), who used the term 'la réalité virtuelle' in his 1938 essay collection *Le Théâtre et son double* to describe the illusory nature of characters and objects on stage. The 1958 English translation of this work represents the first published use of the term 'virtual reality'.

Virtual reality pioneer Morton Heilig (1926-97) wrote on the concept of 'experience theatre' during the 1950s, before patenting the Sensorama in 1962. This was a mechanical device in which the user watched a film on a screen through a viewing portal while their senses were manipulated by a series of appropriate stimuli, such as scents and breeze. It was a financial disaster.

antonin artaud le théâtre et son double

idees gallimard

As computer technology advanced, US tech giant Atari briefly ran a virtual reality research lab from 1982. This was the period in which the term was popularised, and rapidly developing virtual reality technology was used across medical, military, motor and flight simulation applications.

Today, virtual reality is used extensively in the video game industry, with virtual packages available for all major consoles. Given the rate at which virtual reality technology is advancing, it's surely only a matter of time before *Doctor Who* fans can step out of the real world and through the TARDIS doors into a virtual world that is indistinguishable from reality.

This is perhaps the purest representation of a virtual reality in the *Doctor Who* universe – and it goes further. After Donna sacrifices herself to save those trapped in the CAL hard drive, the Doctor uploads River Song's data-ghost into the now repaired system, where River's soul – and those of her dead crew – live on in a virtual world within the computer.

Of all the virtual, augmented-world generating systems, it's the Matrix of Gallifrey that is still shrouded in the secrecy typical of the Time Lords. The Matrix is made up of "trillions of electrochemical cells in a continuous matrix. The cells are the repository of departed Time Lords," Co-ordinator Engin explains to the Doctor in *The Deadly Assassin* (1976). The Doctor was among the first Time Lords to venture into this repository, entering through a mind-link to do battle with Chancellor Goth. Anybody penetrating this realm finds themselves in a nightmarish virtual reality, the landscape able to be altered and influenced by a suitably powerful mind.

"I deny this reality! The reality is a computation matrix," says the defiant Doctor. Goth's retort: "You are trapped in my creation, Doctor. My reality rules!" The traumatic experiences of those within the Matrix have a direct effect on their bodies in the physical world.

Under extreme circumstances, individuals have entered the micro-universe of the Matrix by direct physical means through a network of doors. During his second trial, the Doctor uses the "seventh door", located on the Gallifreyan court space station, to pursue the Valeyard into the Matrix (*The Trial of a Time Lord*, 1986). These doors are opened by means of a key, guarded by the Keeper of the Matrix.

"WHAT YOU SEE AROUND YOU IS NOTHING MORE THAN A VIRTUAL REALITY."
MISS EVANGELISTA

It's even possible to pilot a TARDIS into the Matrix, as the Master does to monitor the Doctor's trial. As with his earlier experiences inside the Matrix, the Doctor finds the Valeyard has engineered the virtual reality to his own mental whims, creating a bizarre steampunk Victorian factory, from which he intends to launch an attack on the High Council of the Time Lords.

Matrix technology is also highly portable, with Matrix 'data slices' able to be removed as one would a computer hard drive. It's within one of these data slices that Missy creates the Nethersphere, an environment to which she uploads the minds of deceased humans, before they're rewritten and uploaded into the waiting bodies of Cybermen (*Dark Water/Death in Heaven*, 2014). Among the virtual environments created within the Nethersphere is a walled garden, a tea room and office space. The ethical atrocities committed by Missy on this occasion are an extreme instance of virtual technology being abused for pure evil.

The reality generated within the Matrix is a side effect of the system's many uses and represents the state of the art in augmented reality generation. The quest to blur the lines between physical and virtual continues...

Above left: The Doctor (Tom Baker) decides to enter the Matrix in *The Deadly Assassin* (1976).

Above right: Missy (Michelle Gomez) welcomes the recently deceased Gretchen (Laura dos Santos) to the Nethersphere in *Into the Dalek* (2014).

Below: Donna experiences a full and happy virtual life with her virtual children. Josh (Alex Midwood) and Ella (Eloise Rakic-Platt) in *Forest of the Dead* (2008) – but she knows that something is wrong.

WEAPONS

From death rays to delta waves, via living plastic and nuclear missiles, *Doctor Who* has presented a chilling array of advanced weaponry.

FEATURE BY **ROBERT FAIRCLOUGH**

In its first two stories, *Doctor Who* ran the gamut of weaponry from the extremely primitive to the ultra-sophisticated – a stone knife (*100,000 BC* aka *An Unearthly Child*, 1963) and Dalek gun-sticks (*The Mutants* aka *The Daleks*, 1963-64). Since then, the series has been replete with any number of stasers, blasters, web guns and heat weapons, as well as conventional Earth armaments such as swords, knives, and the small and heavy ordnance used by Earth defenders UNIT. At various times in *Doctor Who*'s history, weapons have also been central to its stories, reflecting either contemporary scientific development or, most often, fears about sophisticated technology.

Among the most commonly used devices in the series are 'death rays' or laser beams. Popularised as long ago as 1897 via the Martian heat rays used in HG Wells' *The War of the Worlds*, these weapons are a science-fiction staple, arguably because scientists have strived to make them a reality since the 1920s. Laser stands for 'light amplification by stimulated emission of radiation', and the first one to appear in *Doctor Who* was fired by the Cybermen at *The Moonbase* (1967).

The following year, during another Cyberman incursion in *The Wheel in Space*, laser hardware became a major part of Earth's space exploration programme. With a 'thermal blast', the artillery-sized X-ray laser housed in a space station can eliminate hazards such as meteorite swarms and abandoned rockets. Linking it to the TARDIS' Time Vector Generator rod, the Second Doctor is able to increase its power to the level where it can destroy a Cyberman spacecraft.

Perhaps inevitably, such advanced weapons are often harnessed by unscrupulous elements. In *The Monster of Peladon* (1974), what the Doctor describes as "a simple matter projector linked to a directional heat ray" is used by agents of Galaxy 5 to disrupt trisilicate mining. In *Robot* (1974-75), the fascistic Scientific Reform Society steals the technology to assemble a Disintegrator Gun. The Doctor tells the Brigadier that this weapon has "almost unlimited" power and can "drill a hole in the surface of the Moon." Used by the experimental robot K1, the gun plays a key role in the SRS's campaign of global nuclear blackmail.

Bringing the heat ray back to its orgins with a brief mention of HG Wells, *Horror of Fang Rock* (1977) shows how an amplified carbon oscillator can be improvised from the arc beam of a lighthouse. Using a diamond as a focusing device, the resulting emission destroys a Rutan mothership. The 2006 story *Tooth and Claw* is set in the 1870s and depicts a more calculating use of light refracted through a diamond to destroy an alien invader.

THE MOST USED DEVICES IN THE SERIES ARE 'DEATH RAYS' OR LASER BEAMS.

The father of Sir Robert Macleish builds a bogus telescope into the roof of Torchwood House – in reality a prism-filled light chamber that's a trap for a werewolf. Moonlight is beamed from the device through Queen Victoria's Koh-i-Noor diamond, creating a ray powerful enough to obliterate the monster.

Doctor Who has also explored more unusual weapons-grade applications, such as mental energy, chemicals and plastic. An accidental side-effect of Professor Watkins' Cerebration Mentor (*The Invasion*, 1968) is the generation of 'emotion pulses', turning ▶

Opposite page: The Doctor (Christopher Eccleston) sets up a deadly delta wave in *The Parting of the Ways* (2005).

Above: K1 wields the Disintegrator Gun in *Robot* (1974-75).

Below left: The beam from a lighthouse destroys a Rutan mothership in *Horror of Fang Rock* (1977).

Below right: The Cybermen prepare to fire their laser at *The Moonbase* (1967).

◀ a compact, portable teaching machine into a device lethal to the emotionless Cybermen. In a similar vein, 1971's *The Mind of Evil* has the Master exploiting the powers of a mind parasite hidden in his Keller Machine, using it to create fatal hallucinations.

The Krotons (1968-69) are creatures whose biology is based on the crystalline element tellurium; using 'dispersion units' they release a billowing vapour which can reduce flesh, bone and clothing to a crystal-like residue. When attacked by a Kroton with a portable dispersion unit, the TARDIS automatically uses its Hostile Action Displacement System to relocate. Another mineral-based weapon, the distinctively named 'glitter gun',

is mentioned in *Revenge of the Cybermen* (1975). Using the reserves of Voga, the planet of gold, human scientists ended the Cyberwar by inventing a firearm that plated Cybermen's breathing apparatus and suffocated them. An ancestor of the glitter gun may possibly have been the gold-tipped bullets devised by UNIT, as seen in *Battlefield* (1989).

The Master has employed various armaments, ranging through revolvers, laser guns and screwdrivers, and especially the Tissue Compression Eliminator. His collaborators have included the Nestenes, who seem to share his black humour. During their joint campaign in *Terror of the Autons* (1971), the allies variously use a plastic chair, troll doll, phone cable and daffodils, all of which suffocate their victims and are animated by the Nestenes' unique ability to turn plastic into quasi-organic matter.

If there's one form of technophobia that has run through

THE MORE POWERFUL THE WEAPON IN *DOCTOR WHO*, THE GREATER THE ETHICAL DEBATE.

Doctor Who since the beginning, it's anxiety about nuclear weapons. In the first Dalek story, the effects of a conflict that many people saw as the inevitable outcome of the Cold War between the West and the Eastern Bloc could be seen on the planet Skaro – soil turned to ash, petrified life forms and horrific mutations.

The double-edged nature of nuclear weapons is explored in *The Tenth Planet* (1966), when General Cutler plans to fire the Z-Bomb at Mondas. This doomsday weapon might obliterate the rogue planet with what scientist Barclay calls "a terrific blast of radiation", but it might also destroy all life on the side of the Earth facing the explosion; luckily, Ben is able to sabotage it. In 1968's *The Dominators*, nuclear power is presented as a tool of conquest. It powers the Dominators' space fleet, necessitating an attempt to turn the planet Dulkis into a mass of radioactive fuel. Two stories later, atomic weapons were shown in a more positive light. In *The Invasion*, missile batteries from the UK's Hemlow Downs base and – significantly – a Russian warhead destroy both the Cybermen's fleet and a Cyber-Megatron Bomb. As the 1970s dawned, atomic pessimism only grew. In both *The Mind of Evil* (1971) and *Day of the Daleks* (1972) there is a sense of

Top left: A weapon disguised as a telescope is used against a werewolf in *Tooth and Claw* (2006).

Top right: The Thunderbolt nerve-gas missile that is central to the Master's plan in *The Mind of Evil* (1971).

Above: McDermott (Harry Towb) is engulfed by a deadly plastic chair in *Terror of the Autons* (1971).

Right: A Kroton armed with a dispersion unit in *The Krotons* (1968-69).

SMALL WORLD

Somewhere on his travels the Master acquired the grisly technology of 'matter condensation', which fatally shrinks its targets to the size of a doll. Not named on screen as a Tissue Compression Eliminator until 1982's *Time-Flight*, the technique was introduced in *Terror of the Autons* (1971) via a slim, retracting tube which lit up at one end when activated. In this story the device serves the Master's macabre sense of humour when he leaves the shrunken body of the technician Goodge in his own lunch box.

After the Master absorbs the body of Traken's Councillor Tremas, the TCE becomes the renegade Time Lord's weapon of choice. The "nasty little toy" is remodelled as a slender black rod ending in a tulip-shaped head that splits into four parts when ready for firing, exposing a bright light when activated. Humans, Logopolitans and Xeraphin are all among the device's victims, while three regenerations of the Doctor have a lucky escape in *The Five Doctors* (1983).

The TCE can also shrink inorganic material, namely protective suits and the robot Kamelion (*Planet of Fire*, 1984). The weapon's effect on Time Lord technology is variable. Used on the Fifth Doctor's Zero Cabinet in *Castrovalva* (1982) it's apparently ineffective. However, the Doctor is able to sabotage the Master's TARDIS with the TCE in 1983's *The King's Demons* by leaving it activated, a ploy which won't "do his dimension circuits much good". By *The Mark of the Rani* (1985), the TCE can also apparently be used as a gun, destroying a dog and making a guard vanish.

international crisis around China's participation (or not) in two peace conferences, a situation which comes dangerously close to a Third World War. By *Robot*, the SRS is able to steal destructor codes that the Brigadier warns might "set off every atomic missile in the world".

This anxiety continued into the 1980s, with two stories speculating that intervention by a third force could start an atomic war: in *Warriors of Deep* (1984), Silurians and Sea Devils combine in an effort to trigger what the Doctor describes as a nuclear "final solution", while in *Battlefield* (1989) the sorceress Morgaine tries to detonate a nuclear missile. *Cold War* (2013) has a similar scenario, when the stranded Ice Warrior Grand Marshal Skaldak threatens armageddon from the Russian submarine *Firebird*.

The more powerful the weapon in *Doctor Who*, the greater the ethical debate around it. *Colony in Space* (1971) presents the Third Doctor with what was, for a long time, the most destructive device seen in the series. Based on the planet Uxarieus, the Doomsday Weapon can focus on any star in the universe and make it explode. Offered a share in universal domination by the Master, the Doctor firmly states that "absolute power is evil." The Fourth Doctor takes a comparable position when confronted with *Meglos* (1980), who has invented the screens of Zolfa-Thura: the "five beams they throw out can be made to converge on any point in the galaxy, [blasting it] to infinitesimal dust". Put in charge of a similarly destructive force, a delta wave in *The Parting of the Ways* (2005) which can destroy millions of humans and Daleks, the Ninth Doctor is in no doubt where his moral duty lies – even if he can't ultimately trigger a tide of energy that "fries your brain".

It's worth remembering that after Torchwood destroy a retreating Sycorax ship with energy beams in *The Christmas Invasion* (2005), the furious Doctor is able to depose Prime Minister Harriet Jones with just four words. However simple or sophisticated the weapons in *Doctor Who*, it's the morality behind their use that is always the crucial factor.

Top left: One of the saucers from the Dominators' space fleet in *The Dominators* (1968).

Above left: The Master (Roger Delgado) demonstrates the Doomsday Weapon to the Doctor (Jon Pertwee) in *Colony in Space* (1971).

Top right: The Master (Anthony Ainley) uses his tissue compression eliminator on the Doctor's Zero Cabinet in *Castrovalva* (1982).

Above right: The Master (Roger Delgado) activates his tissue compression eliminator in *Terror of the Autons*.

Right: The Doctor (Peter Davison) tries to prevent the Silurians and Sea Devils from triggering a nuclear war in *Warriors of Deep* (1984).

Far right: Captain Zhukov (Liam Cunningham), the Russian commander in change of the submarine *Firebird* in *Cold War* (2013).

THE SCIENCE OF MAGIC

Doctor Who has often favoured pseudo-scientific explanations for events that could otherwise be explained by magic. In 1975, one of its leading writers decided to apply this rule to an episode that had already been broadcast.

FEATURE BY **MARCUS HEARN**

In 1966, the departure of William Hartnell prompted much debate about the future of *Doctor Who*. When it was eventually decided that the series should continue with a new leading man, the production team prepared a document describing how this transformation might be achieved.

The word 'regeneration' would not be used in *Doctor Who* until 1974, but the document has an otherwise clear description of the Doctor's ordeal: 'The metaphysical change which takes place over 500 or so years is a horrifying experience – an experience in which he relives some of the most unendurable moments of his long life, including the galactic war. It is as if he has had the LSD drug and instead of experiencing the kicks, he has the hell and the dank horror which can be its effect.'

"The regeneration was inspired directly from *Dr Jekyll and Mr Hyde*," remembered story editor Gerry Davis. "A simple inspiration to get the changeover between actors."

Working with Kit Pedler, Davis had completed his original draft of *The Tenth Planet*, the First Doctor's final regular story, before it had been confirmed that Hartnell was leaving. By the time Episode 4 was recorded at Riverside Studios on 8 October 1966, Davis had bolted on a new closing sequence where the frail old Doctor collapses on the floor of the TARDIS control room. As an incredulous Ben (Michael Craze) and Polly (Anneke Wills) look on, the Doctor's face is bathed in bright light. His features eventually resolve into those of an entirely different man – namely Hartnell's replacement, Patrick Troughton.

Nine years later, Davis was asked to adapt *The Tenth Planet* for Target Books' burgeoning range of *Doctor Who* novelisations. Davis had long since relinquished his story-editing post and had reportedly turned down the opportunity to produce the series, but he accepted the commission and delivered a manuscript that contains a number of intriguing changes from the broadcast version. Not least among these was the Doctor's regeneration.

Presumably unsatisfied by the essentially unexplained nature of the Doctor's transformation, Davis decided to introduce a machine to aid the process. In the final pages of the book, Ben and Polly hear an unfamiliar cry in the TARDIS control room. They rush over to 'a long couch-like arrangement with a folding metal cover over it. The use of it had never been fully explained to them. The Doctor had simply told them that it compressed sleep. The cry seemed to be coming from this apparatus.'

In Davis' book, the transformation takes place entirely out of sight, while the Doctor is encased in this device. Polly struggles with a catch that she hopes will open it, before Ben activates a lever that reveals 'a long, stretcher-like couch.'

Davis then describes the middle-aged man who emerges from the machine. 'The Doctor's long, silver locks had been replaced by short dark hair, and the newcomer had a swarthy, almost gypsy, appearance.'

Davis belonged to an era of the programme where sound – or at least plausible – scientific principles underpinned much of the storytelling, so it's perhaps unsurprising that he felt the need to augment the magic of regeneration with his 'sleeping compressor'.

It's not clear whether this device first appeared in a (now lost) draft of Davis' *Tenth Planet* scripts or whether it was invented for the Target book. The latter explanation seems less probable, given that the series had already featured three 'traditional' regenerations by the time Davis' book was published in February 1976.

If the machine was indeed a remnant from one of Davis' unused scripts, this may explain why Ben remains so sceptical that the new Doctor is the genuine article when the next story, *The Power of the Daleks*, begins – even though in the televised version of *The Tenth Planet* he's actually witnessed the transformation. It may also explain why, in *The Power of the Daleks* Episode One, the new Doctor explains that the process is "part of the TARDIS. Without it I wouldn't survive…"

One thing is certain, however: if Arthur C Clarke was correct, and sufficiently advanced technology really is indistinguishable from magic, then this was an instance of *Doctor Who* using one to explain the other.

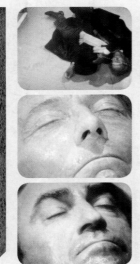

Top: Gerry Davis co-wrote *The Tenth Planet* in 1966 and was commissioned to novelise the story nine years later.

Above right: *Doctor Who and the Tenth Planet* was first published by Target Books on 19 February 1976.

Right: The Doctor (William Hartnell) regenerates without the use of a machine in Episode 4 of *The Tenth Planet* (1966).

Far right: Ben (Michael Craze) and Polly (Anneke Wills) are suspicious of the new Doctor (Patrick Troughton) in *The Power of the Daleks* Episode One (1966).